SAYING NO TO SAY YES

SAYING NO TO SAY YES

Everyday Boundaries and Pastoral Excellence

David C. Olsen and Nancy G. Devor

An Alban Institute Book

ROWMAN & LITTLEFIELD
Lanham • Boulder • New York • London

Published by Rowman & Littlefield
A wholly owned subsidiary of The Rowman & Littlefield Publishing
Group, Inc.
4501 Forbes Boulevard, Suite 200, Lanham, Maryland 20706
www.rowman.com

Unit A, Whitacre Mews, 26-34 Stannary Street, London SE11 4AB

British Library Cataloguing in Publication Information Available

Library of Congress Cataloging-in-Publication Data

Olsen, David C., 1952–
Saying no to say yes : everyday boundaries and pastoral excellence / David C. Olsen and
Nancy G. Devor.
pages cm
Includes bibliographical references and index.
ISBN 978-1-56699-767-6 (cloth : alk. paper)—ISBN 978-1-56699-728-7 (pbk. : alk.
paper)—ISBN 978-1-56699-729-4 (electronic)
1. Clergy—Psychology. 2. Clergy—Mental health. I. Title.
BV4398.O47 2015
253'.2—dc23

2014043964

∞™ The paper used in this publication meets the minimum requirements
of American National Standard for Information Sciences Permanence of
Paper for Printed Library Materials, ANSI/NISO Z39.48-1992.

Printed in the United States of America

CONTENTS

INTRODUCTION

Writing about boundaries—or how to set limits, both personally and professionally—is a daunting endeavor. The lack of professional boundaries among clergy whose misconduct has been splashed across national newspapers has inflicted horrific pain on the individuals affected and betrayed far too many congregations. But most clergy don't engage in the notorious violations reported in the daily news. Though we may not realize it, we likely face more mundane boundary challenges every day, from being called to attend an emergency sickbed during our child's music performance to the unspoken expectation that we attend every committee meeting. We may be worn down by the demands of ministry, disconnected from the source of energy that inspired our call and that nurtures our gifts. Could depletion and burnout also be caused by a lack of boundaries?

This book discusses the ordinary boundary problems that are robbing too many clergy and congregations from life-giving ministry. Our hope is that the book will help readers move beyond generic suggestions for boundary setting, such as "take more time for yourself" or "request a sabbatical," to a much deeper understanding of where boundary challenges come from, how we react to them, and how we can work with ourselves, our families, and our congregations to set boundaries that reinvigorate ministry.

Chapter 1 provides an overview of the scope of the problem. Even though clergy sexual misconduct (CSM) is not the major concern of this book, reviewing the problem of CSM helps us understand the factors that lead to many types of boundary problems—and also how boundary training was initiated as a response to the egregious violations of clergy sexual misconduct.

We believe a different type of boundary training that moves beyond sexual-misconduct problems could be more helpful to most clergy who struggle with quite ordinary and vexing dilemmas. In chapters 2, 3, and 4, we set the context for this different type of boundary training. Chapter 2 addresses the self-deficits clergy bring into ministry that can interfere with setting limits. The lens of self psychology, which helps us view our need for affirmation, offers one way to see the deficits that can interfere with setting appropriate limits. In chapter 3, we use another lens—Bowenian family-systems theory—to explore the resistance of the systems in which clergy operate and how systems impact our ability to set boundaries. Chapter 4 considers the interaction effect of the intrapersonal factors of clergy and the systemic factors in which we operate—and how that interaction effect makes setting boundaries even more complicated. With an understanding of obstacles that block our capacity to set limits, we can turn to the task of change. In chapter 5, we review recent discussions of "pastoral excellence" as we remember our call and what inspired us to enter the ministry. Then we turn to notions of self-differentiation and emotional intelligence for practical advice as we negotiate saying "no" to say "yes" to the life-giving practices that nurture pastoral excellence.

HOW TO USE THIS BOOK

We wrote this book with the hope that it could be used in multiple ways. Individual clergy may read this book to deepen their understanding and practice in setting boundaries. We include practice sections at the end of chapters 1–4 and throughout chapter 5 to offer a springboard for reflection, discussion, and change.

Professional facilitators may use the content of this book to teach boundary training for groups of clergy. Appendix 1 includes an outline that can be adapted for four- or eight-hour workshops. Workshop goals include presenting a comprehensive overview of boundary issues and introducing participants to the task of setting clear boundaries. But boundary-awareness trainings only allow time for an overview of some very complicated concepts. At the end of an eight-hour presentation, clergy have been challenged to think differently about boundaries. However, thinking about boundaries is quite different from implementing a different way of doing ministry.

To fully implement these concepts as a step toward pastoral excellence, a far more intensive process is necessary. We are strong advocates of participating in facilitated clergy groups. We believe that the best way to integrate the concepts introduced in this book and workshops based on this material is to use the book in a clergy group where the concepts can be carefully explored, discussed, and implemented. The concepts presented in this book are both difficult and potentially life changing. Applying these concepts to our personal and professional lives with the support and challenge of an excellent clergy group can be tremendously helpful.

Why are clergy groups so effective? A group with a structured curriculum and a trained facilitator provides a place where clergy feel safe and supported yet are challenged to learn and improve. Offering both support and challenge, clergy peer-learning groups could be an ideal format to consider the topic of boundaries as discussed in this book. Tips for how to start a clergy group are included in appendix 2.

We wrote this book because of our own personal and professional experiences. We've learned about the personal wounds and family roles within ourselves and our families of origin that have made it difficult for us to set limits, and we've watched many clergy struggle with similar issues. Out of our personal experiences, our professional interest has grown: David has provided boundary-awareness workshops for over fifteen years across the New York and New England region. Nancy has led clergy consultation groups as well as an eight-year program funded by the Lilly Endowment focused on teaching Samaritan Counseling Center staff throughout the country how to offer care for clergy and congregations.

Writing about boundaries is daunting—but learning to practice personal and professional limits in the setting of ministry may reinvigorate your life and the life of your congregation. We invite you to say "no" to say "yes" to the life-giving call of ministry.

1

THE PROBLEM WITH BOUNDARIES

Too often when boundary problems are discussed, worst-case examples come to mind. And the worst-case examples invariably involve sexual misconduct: a minister becomes sexually involved with a parishioner who comes for counseling, a youth director becomes too involved in the lives of teenagers, a minister is found to have pornography on the church's computer. While these are examples of boundary problems that are sadly too frequent, they are in some ways unhelpful examples. Because so much time and energy goes into dealing with these notorious examples, everyday boundary problems among clergy are rarely talked about. The reality is that setting and maintaining clear boundaries for clergy is often complicated by long-term neglect of personal and professional needs and limits, as the following two examples demonstrate.

Robert, a tall, well-dressed senior minister from a tall-steeple church, slumped dejectedly into a chair in my office. Despite his professional appearance, his affect was flat, and he seemed to have little energy. He announced in a rather lifeless voice that he was burned out and then smiled and said, "I'm not sure I even know what that means." While he enjoyed a successful long-term tenure in a progressive congregation, he described his ministry as lifeless and flat and stated that he was simply going through the motions at this point. He reported being distracted, bored, and agitated. The energy and idealism from earlier in his ministry that allowed him to work long hours had faded. He reported dread of board meetings and even disliked the sound of his own voice when preaching.

He acknowledged that he no longer keeps up with serious reading, watches too much TV, and admitted with some embarrassment that he looks forward to getting home, watching mindless TV, and drinking wine—and revealed that he is drinking more wine than ever. He noted that he is not sure how he is going to make it to retirement. He stated that spiritually he feels empty and often feels like a fraud while preaching.

For years, Robert has worked sixty- and seventy-hour weeks, has taken little time off, and has added significant responsibility in his judicatory. Robert has ignored boundaries and self-care for decades. He has never taken time for himself and his own spiritual life. He has found it difficult to say "no" on too many occasions, resulting in being chronically overcommitted and having difficulty even knowing what he needs. What he didn't realize was the absence of healthy boundaries in his work life and his inability to say "no" resulted in burnout and even depression.

Sandra, on the other hand, is a younger version of Robert. Sandra had been called to the congregation she was serving because the search committee was looking for an energetic younger minister to revitalize their congregation and help them return to the glory years when the Sunday school was booming and the pews were full. Despite major changes in the community, an aging congregation, and the downsizing of several key employers in town, the expectation was that Sandra could create growth. And in her idealism, she agreed to take on the assignment. She worked tirelessly, launched new programs, and experimented with new worship forms, only to face increased criticism from the older members of the congregation. The congregation, unprepared for the very changes they stated they desired, became increasingly anxious, and so did she. Sandra wanted desperately to succeed. At the same time, she was running on empty.

In addition to her work, Sandra was married and had a young child. Whether at home or at work, someone always wanted something from Sandra. Fighting fatigue, she stopped exercising and praying and gave in to eating fast food on the run. With no time to think through requests and respond thoughtfully, a cycle of reactivity began spiraling out of control. Instead of being free to choose her response, Sandra began to internalize requests as non-negotiable demands. As requests were made, Sandra reacted—often with an undertone of anger. The congregation or her family members criticized her response, and Sandra became increasingly defensive and aggressive in tone, which only served to increase the complaints.

Sandra, while defensive and anxious, knew problems were brewing. What she did not realize was that her depletion, anxiety, and desperate need for validation had provided fertile ground for a culture of criticism and complaint. At the beginning of psychotherapy, she had no idea how much she longed for validation and how hard she would work to get it, rather than stepping back and setting limits on much-needed time for reflection and self-care.

Both Robert and Sandra are dealing with significant problems that result from lack of clear boundaries. While their stories are different, both are struggling because of their inability to understand and establish clear boundaries in their respective ministries and to find authentic sources of personal and professional replenishment.

WHAT ARE BOUNDARIES?

Too often boundaries are viewed as negative restrictions, rather than limits that promote and contribute to health (we use the terms "boundaries" and "limits" interchangeably). In one of the first stories in the Bible, God sets a "boundary" in the Garden of Eden. God offers freedom to live our lives within the context of a limit. The story does not end well. As Adam and Eve cross the boundary, innocence and freedom are disrupted, and we see in the story the beginning of shame, guilt, and alienation. Could this be a paradigmatic story for ministry? Is it possible that freedom is always lost when boundaries are violated and that setting and maintaining healthy boundaries unleashes new energy for pastoral excellence?

Paradoxically, limits are necessary for human growth and flourishing. For example, healthy marriages set certain boundaries around the relationship, for without the safety of healthy boundaries, intimacy cannot flourish. Marital boundaries, or vows, are intended to increase intimacy and love. When they are crossed, intense pain, betrayal, and alienation result.

Healthy families also understand that boundaries are essential for effective child development. Research suggests that healthy parents set limits that are not too rigid or too loose but are aimed at being developmentally appropriate so children are free to be children, are safe, and do not have to take care of their parents. Unhealthy families, such as families organized around alcoholism, often do not maintain effective boundaries. Children raised in families without limits grow up feeling excessively burdened. As the result of addiction, often one or more of the children are "parentified" and have to take on the role of caregiver, feeling over-responsible for almost everything.

The absence of healthy boundaries often saddles those who grow up in alcoholic families with lifelong anxiety. As adults, these individuals recall feeling pressured to keep their parents sober, make sure there was enough money, and provide meals and protection for their younger siblings. To no surprise, they also report feeling hyper-vigilant, over-responsible, and unable to relax. These are the unfortunate results of growing up without healthy boundaries.

While boundaries are essential for producing family health—and much of couple and family therapy focuses on creating a clear structure and boundaries for the well-being of the couple and family— they are also essential for physical health. Physicians prescribe health boundaries to help their patients move toward wellness. Most of us have heard the basic medical advice: watch what you eat, exercise, do not smoke, and so forth. None of this advice is meant to be negative, just as parents do not set clear boundaries to ruin their kids' fun. Good boundaries aim at producing health.

On the simplest level, boundaries define the separation between self and other. A person with a healthy sense of self knows what he or she wants and needs and is able to say "no" to what is not helpful and request more of what he or she needs. As we've noted above, without clear personal boundaries, healthy relationships are very difficult. Physical boundaries define how close someone can become, who can touch us, and how that person can touch us. Emotional boundaries are more complicated. Discerning our emotions and how they are separate from the feelings of those around us is not always clear. Sometimes we take responsibility for what another feels and then try to give her what she needs without even stopping to reflect on what we might need. Saying "no" in the territory of emotional needs can be difficult, especially if we have a need to please people, rescue them, or be the hero. We may default to automatic roles, without considering our boundaries.

While boundaries can be too permeable, they can also be too rigid. The most obvious example of boundaries that are too permeable is clergy sexual abuse, but others are more ordinary and problematic. As Margaret Marcuson points out in her book *Leaders Who Last: Sustaining Yourself and Your Ministry*, avoiding conflict by never taking a stand or limiting your social life to your parishioners so that you are too close to take a stand are also problematic, too-permeable boundaries. But being too rigid is also problematic. Some clergy set limits and boundaries in such a way that people feel alienated and pushed away. Marcuson points out the problem of distancing by avoiding others or becoming distracted so that our relationships are not substantive enough to allow us to lead. Clergy who distance or hold too-rigid boundaries forget that healthy boundaries are meant to allow healthy intimacy. Boundaries that are too inflexible block people from connecting and getting close.

Robert Frost is famous for the line "good fences make good neighbors," a way of talking about the value of boundaries.[1] But in another less-well-known poem, "There Are Roughly Zones," Frost talks about the problems caused by our human tendency to over-reach our boundaries. The context for the poem is a bitterly cold night in northern New England. We overhear a conversation about a peach tree—and how it was "very far north" to plant a tree that can't withstand such cold. "If it never again has leaves, / We'll know, we say, that this was the night it died."[2] Drawing on this metaphor of a peach tree on a cold winter's night, Frost asks why humans seem incapable of staying within discrete limits or boundaries. He asks why it is so hard for humans to learn that even though there isn't a "fixed line between wrong and right," "there are roughly zones whose laws must be obeyed?" In the same way that a peach tree planted outside its hardiness zone will die on a cold winter night, humans without boundaries can also perish. Boundaries are the "laws" protecting those "rough zones" that, when ignored, contribute to and result from an ongoing cycle of burnout and lack of limits and, in the worst case, clergy sexual misconduct. But when we learn to live within limits, boundaries lead to life and flourishing ministries.

CLERGY SEXUAL MISCONDUCT

The most egregious and most studied result of poor boundaries is in the area of clergy sexual misconduct (CSM). While CSM is not the focus of this book—and indeed, our perspective is that focusing on CSM in boundary training obscures the ordinary boundary dilemmas facing most clergy—nevertheless, a brief review of CSM research underscores the need for attention to boundaries.

Most of the studies regarding the prevalence of clergy sexual misconduct have been self-report surveys that have found incidents of misconduct occurring in as few as 1 percent and as many as 15 percent of various clergy samples.[3] The most thorough research to date has been conducted by Duke University professor of sociology Mark Chaves and Dean Diana Garland of Baylor School of Social Work (2009).[4] They added a subset of questions about clergy sexual misconduct to the 2008 General Social Survey (GSS), a representative national random survey. So instead of employing the traditional method of surveying clergy about their behavior, Chaves and Garland turned to the survivor-victims of misconduct. In particular, they asked the survey participants whether, since they had turned eighteen years of age, they had experienced "sexual advances or propositions" from a religious leader who was not a spouse or significant other. Their findings indicated that of those surveyed:

- More than 3 percent of women who had attended a congregation in the past month reported that they had been the object of CSM [clergy sexual misconduct] at some time in their adult lives;

- 92 percent of these sexual advances had been made in secret, not in open dating relationships; and
- 67 percent of the offenders were married to someone else at the time of the advance.
- In the average American congregation of four hundred persons, with women representing, on average, 60 percent of the congregation, there are, on [sic] average of seven women who have experienced clergy sexual misconduct.
- Of the entire sample, 8 percent report having known about CSM occurring in a congregation they have attended. Therefore, in the average American congregation of four hundred persons, there are, on average, thirty-two persons who have experienced CSM in their community of faith.[5]

Two other research findings emphasize the breadth of the problem of clergy sexual misconduct. First, research by Garland and Christen Argueta, a Baylor University research associate, found that clergy sexual misconduct occurs in many denominations and religious faiths. They conducted a qualitative study of forty-six persons who as adults experienced a sexual advance by a religious leader. In their study, seventeen different Christian and Jewish affiliations were represented among congregations experiencing CSM.[6] Second, in the GSS survey mentioned above, an additional disturbing finding was that African American women were more likely than Caucasian women to have experienced clergy sexual misconduct. When asked whether they knew of friends or family members who experienced a sexual advance by a religious leader in their congregation, 8.5 percent of African Americans and 3.7 percent of Caucasians answered affirmatively.[7] Taken together, these studies show us that the problem of clergy sexual misconduct is not limited to any denomination or racial group, and that while the media may focus on Roman Catholic priests abusing young boys, the reality is that too many women—and African American women in particular—are survivor-victims.

While the literature reports instances of female offenders, in the GSS study all of the offenders were male, and 96 percent of the offended were female.[8] We can extrapolate from this data to hypothesize that men and women may have different issues regarding boundaries and that training needs to target the needs of men and women differentially, as we will discuss in chapter 5.

With the ever-increasing cost of clergy-sexual-abuse litigation, denominations have instituted policies identifying sexual relations between adult congregants and clergy as misconduct subject to discipline.[9] In July 2010, the General Assembly of the Presbyterian Church (U.S.A.) approved an amendment to require all governing bodies in the denomination to have a sexual-misconduct policy. Other judicatories have begun to require clergy to attend boundary workshops. For example, in the experience of the authors, the Vermont Conference of the United Church of Christ requires periodic updating of boundary training for all active clergy, and we have been invited to conduct mandatory boundary training for Presbyterian, United Church of Christ, United Methodist, and other denominational groups, as well as Catholic Charities.

CLERGY BURNOUT

While clergy-sexual-misconduct statistics are sobering, they tell only part of the story. Another significant problem is clergy burnout. How are they related? Poor boundaries certainly are a primary factor contributing to burnout, and burnout makes us less careful about maintaining healthy boundaries. Many times, poor boundaries and burnout go together.

The statistics for burnout among clergy are as alarming as the statistics for CSM. Much of the research on clergy burnout relies on the work of Christina Maslach, one of the pioneering researchers on job burnout. Maslach defines burnout as the presence of at least three symptoms: emotional exhaustion, depersonalization (treating others as objects), and feelings of a lack of personal accomplishment at work.[10]

A 2007 study of United Methodist clergy in the New York Annual Conference found that 19 percent reported high emotional exhaustion, 10 percent high depersonalization, and 11 percent low personal accomplishment, echoing the results of a 2004 study of a cohort of Anglican priests.[11] A 2004 study of Roman Catholic priests found that 36 percent felt "used up" at the end of the day, 20 percent felt frustrated, 19 percent felt "emotionally drained," and 14 percent identified themselves as burned out.[12] Peter Steinke, well known for his work with clergy and congregations, describes the high level of stress and burnout among clergy in response to significant anxiety in congregational life.[13]

We believe that most clergy are well intentioned, and despite sobering statistics, most are not predators. More often, sexual misconduct and burnout are the painful consequences of the absence of boundaries all along the journey of ministry, and the lack of boundaries contributes to CSM and burnout. Most clergy do not start out burned out or engaging in sexual misconduct, but burnout and CSM become the result of long-standing, unattended needs to be liked and validated and the difficulty clergy experience in saying "no" in multiple environments. While sexual misconduct is a very serious problem, too often other foundational problems—such as the factors leading to professional burnout—are overlooked along the way when boundaries are framed as only pertaining to sexual relationships between clergy and laity.

WHAT CAUSES BOUNDARY PROBLEMS?

Too often in the literature on burnout and boundary problems, writers locate the problem in either the minister or the system, as if burnout and neglected boundaries were an "either/or" proposition. In the following two sections, we'll sample some writers who talk only about intrapersonal causes (those within the clergyperson) and others who discuss only systemic causes (those external to the clergyperson). In the third section, we will discuss our belief that both intrapersonal and systemic factors interact, which is why boundary problems can be so intractable.

Intrapersonal Factors

One body of literature suggests the problem of boundaries lies in the self of the minister and describes some clergy as predators or perfectionists who have a need for control or to be liked. Ironically, the earliest research on burnout suggested the overly dedicated and excessively committed individual is most prone to burnout, theorizing that these persons tend to overextend themselves as a result of their high expectations and idealism.[14] While this proved true in early research on job burnout in various not-for-profit organizations, it is certainly applicable to clergy, who bring to their call a great sense of idealization and commitment.

The ways in which an individual views stress and attempts to reduce it are important factors in the development of burnout. William James anticipated this in his lectures in 1901 and 1902 when he talked about "healthy-mindedness," which he saw as the ability to view things in a basically optimistic way.[15] A study of parish-based clergy found that strategies such as acceptance, active coping, planning, and positive reframing were protective factors against burnout.[16] Yet it is not clear why some people are able to stay positive and others become overwhelmed by stress.

Part of the answer of why some clergy are more resilient in the face of stress may be in a connection between developmental factors and the ability to process stress. If significant life events have worn down their reserve, they find themselves less able to process stress creatively, leading to burnout. Some have proposed that the life stage of the clergyperson impacts his or her capacity to tolerate stress and work effectively. For example, in midlife, he or she may be reexamining life's meaning, attending to a growing dissatisfaction with his or her marriage or roles as a partner, and even struggling to remain generative. With self-awareness and reflection, these midlife issues could lead clergy into conscious and thoughtful choices about their vocation and their relationships and lead to a renewed sense of meaning and purpose. But without self-examination, midlife issues and the associated anxiety to keep them from consciousness can cause clergy to act out in ways that result in poor boundary decisions, even CSM. Not surprisingly, many misconduct issues occur at midlife. One study found that pastors who became involved in extramarital sexual affairs were on average in their early forties.[17]

Systemic Factors

While these intrapersonal theories all have some merit, a second body of literature argues that boundary problems—and the resulting burnout—are the fault of anxious systems. While many clergy like to think they are autonomous and even "differentiated," the reality is we are all embedded in networks of relationships that define and sustain us. Christina Maslach illustrates the perspective that systemic factors trump the multitude of potential intrapersonal factors. She comments, "I am forced by the weight of my research to conclude that the problem [of burnout] is best understood in terms of the social situational sources of job related stress. The prevalence of the phenomenon and the range of seemingly desperate professionals who are affected by it suggest that the search for causes is better directed away from the unending cycle of identifying the 'bad people' and towards uncovering the operational and structural characteristics in the 'bad' situations where many good people function."[18] No matter how stress hardy we are, how well we apply healthy coping strategies so that we can avoid burnout, there's something we can't control: the stress resulting from our vocational settings. So in addition to attending to intrapersonal factors, we also must attend to the complexity of the systems in which we are embedded, the chronic anxiety that is part of some systems, as well as the power of certain systems to create anxiety and burnout.

Many writers describe chronic anxiety in congregations. Certainly the decline occurring in the majority of mainline congregations—and the reality that no one knows what to do about it—results in high anxiety about the future. Holding clear boundaries and practicing self-care in a healthy congregation is hard work, but to do so in a congregational system that is chronically anxious about its future, is experiencing and worried about declining finances, and wants to bring back the glory years of the last generation is an even greater challenge. Setting boundaries as anxiety ratchets up in a congregation becomes increasingly difficult. In this regard, issues of the system become a large contributing factor in boundary problems. Clergy entering declining congregations are usually not prepared for the level of chronic anxiety and the expectations for their performance that the congregation's anxiety brings. Systemic anxiety will be explored in much greater detail in chapter 3.

The Interaction of Intrapersonal and Systemic Factors

Our position is that both intrapersonal and systemic theories help explain boundary problems but do not go far enough independently to fully explain the depth of the problem. We believe that boundary problems occur when issues within the self of the clergy intersect with anxious church systems, creating an additional interaction effect.

The following story shows how the combination of intrapersonal and systemic factors makes a difficult situation worse. The Rev. Martha was called to a small-town parish that could afford only a part-time salary. This arrangement met Martha's desires to spend time with her family. However, her largely unconscious need to be appreciated (which she was not receiving at home) meant that she looked to her congregation for appreciation, and she paid only lip service to saying "no"—working more than full time, providing pastoral care, planning worship, meeting with youth groups, leading adult education, and serving as pastor for the town beyond the congregation. She worked night and day in order to avoid anyone criticizing her.

Despite her best efforts, the church's membership was primarily comprised of elders with few youth, children, or their young parents attending. More and more young families were too busy for church—or attended the nondenominational church in a neighboring town. Parishioners feared losing a way of life—socially, vocationally, and spiritually. When the church building needed major repairs, anxiety erupted in a conflict at a board meeting where Martha felt criticized and blindsided—and thus lashed out at the congregation for whom she was sacrificing so much.

If the parishioners had not been anxious about the feared decline and loss of their congregation, they might have been more appreciative of Martha's efforts. But their anxiety meant that they projected their fears on a close target—someone who, like themselves, was working hard to stay even but was not in control of the outcome. Had Martha had better boundaries—and been more aware of the need to work on her home life so she felt more nurtured personally—she might have been able to be more objective about the conflict and less reactive.

This example illustrates how both parties—pastor and congregation—can turn up the volume, contributing to the increasing anxiety on both sides, rather than helping contain and defuse conflict. Setting boundaries in such a reactive, conflicting, and anxious system was nearly impossible for Martha.

Our goal throughout this book is to show the power of the complex interaction of the intrapersonal factors within clergy and the systemic factors in which clergy are embedded. When unresolved or unconscious issues within clergy intersect with the demands of an anxious congregation, boundary problems are bound to result. For example, what happens to a minister who has a need to be liked, and has high idealism, when serving in a chronically anxious declining system with enormous pastoral expectations? Setting healthy boundaries is anything but easy.

BOUNDARY-AWARENESS TRAINING

As a result of too many stories like those of the clergy described above, in addition to the statistics about clergy sexual misconduct, most denominations have become alarmed about the difficulty clergy have setting and maintaining boundaries and have initiated workshops and training in "boundary awareness."

Historically, boundary-awareness workshops for clergy have been focused quite narrowly. The original motivation driving boundary training was significant sexual misconduct among male clergy and the long-standing tendency of judicatories to both cover it up and relocate clergy to other congregations. Between the significant scandals involving pedophile priests and significant cover-ups of these crimes, as well as mounting evidence of sexual misconduct among clergy in mainline denominations, voices in the church, often representing the many survivor-victims, cried out for change. Mandatory boundary-awareness workshops became a way of dealing with a staggering problem.

What really provided the impetus for boundary-awareness training? Certainly some preventive educational efforts were initiated because of growing denominational awareness and concern. A different view was suggested in a journal article by Timothy Lytton, a professor at Albany Law School. [19] Lytton claims that were it not for litigation, the church would never have cleaned up its act. He asserts that the growing problem of misconduct, along with a lack of effective response from church hierarchies, led victim-survivors to pursue justice in the courts. For too long, the response of both the Catholic Church and mainline Protestant denominations was to cover up abuse or to relocate acting-out clergy. Lytton argues convincingly that judicatory denial would have continued were it not for litigation.

Or maybe the real motivation for boundary training was financial. The Associated Press reported in 2009 that the U.S. Catholic Church alone had paid out more than $2.6 billion since 1950 because of clergy misconduct. [20] Because the church coffers could not survive further clergy sexual abuse lawsuits, a preventive educational effort was suggested by their malpractice carriers as a way to mitigate liability.

Marie Fortune, with her book *Is Nothing Sacred?*, was one of the first to write about the need to deal openly with the problem of clergy sexual misconduct, rather than covering it up or relocating acting-out clergy. Following the lead of secular organizations that had already initiated significant steps by setting up sexual-harassment policies and procedures, Fortune pushed the church to catch up to the rest of the professional world. Even more successful was her initiative in changing the understanding of clergy boundary violations. Usually described as "affairs," Fortune shifted the language, describing clergy who were sexually involved with members of their congregations as guilty of sexual misconduct. She provoked a necessary and significant change in terminology, as well as a change in the conceptual framework for professional relationships, a change sadly still in process among some congregations and denominations.

Fortune was a major force in transforming the church's paradigm for conceptualizing boundary violations. She argued that clergy misconduct should be seen in the same way as it is in other professions, such as social work and psychology, and that its occurrence should result in significant professional censure and discipline. She likened misconduct to incest, since both take place in what should be a safe place and are committed by trusted persons.

In 1977, Fortune founded the Faith Trust Institute to more effectively train clergy to prevent CSM. Her writings and work with the institute led to a workshop and associated workbook that framed the problem of clergy boundary violations as sexual misconduct. Her training was adopted as mandatory for clergy of many judicatories.

Fortune's contributions opened up a problem too often buried by the church and started a dialogue about boundary awareness. The statistics about clergy sexual misconduct provide more than ample support for Fortune's version of boundary training.

While the need for sexual-boundary training is obvious, sexual boundaries are not the most common, or even the most complicated, boundary problems that clergy must deal with day in and day out, at work and at home. Training based on CSM as the paradigm for boundary violations fails clergy and the wider church, ignoring the ordinary situations in which most clergy struggle to set limits so they might engage more fully in the call that brought them to ministry. By neglecting deeper intrapersonal and systemic factors, boundary training can lead us into complacency about clergy and congregational health, as well as to miss an opportunity to enhance clergy and congregational effectiveness and vitality.

For example, consider the multiple roles that clergy are asked to assume within a congregation. Most professions have clearly defined roles and expertise. This in turn gives them authority in their particular context. We expect our CPA to know tax law and give us clear advice and guidance as we fill out our tax forms. We expect our physicians to accurately diagnose and appropriately treat an illness that we report. However, we do not ask our CPA for advice about our health, raising our children, or marriage. Nor do we ask our physician for help preparing our taxes. They each function within a clearly defined scope of practice. In fact, most states have regulatory boards that define the scope of practice for each of the licensed professions, delineating what they have been trained to do and how to file a complaint if they function outside of their scope of practice.

Compare these circumscribed roles of most professions to the roles of many clergy. Clergy are often expected to be generalists with expertise in everything from family and marital problems, to finance, to administration, to preaching, teaching, pastoral care, and spiritual direction—and even occasional janitorial and landscaping duties. In addition, clergy meet with parishioners in a variety of contexts that make boundaries more complicated. Over time, clergy get to know a lot about their parishioners and have to interact with them in multiple contexts. A minister might have an emergency counseling session with a family in crisis, one of whose members is the chair of the finance committee, and then meet up with them again over a church dinner. Not surprisingly then, the contexts in which clergy function are extremely complicated and fluid.

In addition, much of boundary training has failed to recognize that there is a systemic component to boundary problems. In short, clergy are asked to set boundaries in congregational and denominational systems that resist (and resent) boundaries. Too often, congregations are highly anxious, as we will explore in chapter 3, and have demanding expectations for their clergy. Many believe their minister should be on call 24/7. In such congregations, clergy who set boundaries are overriding congregational norms and desires.

With the pressure of internal needs for approval and validation, the system pressures to be on duty 24/7, and the way anxiety on both sides of the equation increases an interaction effect, clergy face difficult odds in setting boundaries, too often saying "yes" to everything. This is especially true in small parishes, where clergy must be generalists and have skills in a wide variety of pastoral tasks, ranging from preaching to pastoral care to administration to making sure the heat is on and the bulletins are printed accurately.

Many clergy report they have far too many bosses, all of whom expect something different, and feel pressured to say "yes" to everything. However, when clergy say "yes" to everything, and have trouble saying "no," mediocrity is the result, and the church suffers. What is often missing in boundary-awareness training is a framework that acknowledges that sexual boundaries, while of course important, are not the only critical boundaries.

Rather, general personal and professional boundaries are essential to any successful, thriving ministry. Without the ability to say "no" and set clear limits in ministry, clergy cannot say "yes" to all that contributes to pastoral excellence. In this sense, we believe that boundaries are the key not only to the prevention of both sexual misconduct and burnout but also to the revitalization of the church. Boundary-awareness training therefore needs to be significantly expanded to focus on boundaries in general if it is to contribute to the revitalization of the church.

While boundary trainings and literature have focused a lot of attention on clergy sexual misconduct, little has been said about the day-to-day problems of setting boundaries in ministry. By focusing on setting limits in anxious systems, we hope to help clergy say "no" to what depletes their health and the health of their congregations in order to say "yes" to the attitudes, knowledge, and skills that promote pastoral excellence and contribute to the overall health of the pastor, the pastor's family, and the congregation.

PRACTICE

1. Recall the last time you said "yes" to a request, spoken or implied, from a member of your congregation and you wanted to say "no."
2. What was the request? What was the context of the request?
3. On a scale of one to ten (ten being high), how much did you regret saying "yes"?
4. How did you feel at the time? Later in the day or week? After you fulfilled the request?
5. What did you say to yourself about the reasons for your choice? How did this storyline impact your feelings about the request?
6. Were you aware of a reaction in your body to the situation? If so, what was it? What did the reaction suggest to you about your feelings about the request?
7. What kinds of compensatory behaviors or "escapism" did you engage in, and what did these behaviors suggest about your feelings and needs?

8. What do you imagine would have happened if you said "no" instead of "yes"?

9. What repercussions might have emerged in the congregational system? How would you handle those reactions?

10. If you had said "no," how do you think you would have felt?

11. If you had said "no," what different "yes" do you think might have been free to emerge? Describe how that different scenario feels.

2

HEALTHY SELVES AND BOUNDARIES

Our limits are frequently self-evident. We all have experienced a time when we hear a request and feel our internal resistance building. Often when we are asked to take on an additional responsibility, our internal answer is, "No way!" Yet out of our mouths comes the phrase, "I'd be glad to help." When we say "yes" when our instinct is to say "no"—depending on our status and the kind of request—we may find ourselves weighed down with regret, agitation, fatigue, and more. On some level, we believe we have let ourselves down.

Recall Pastor Martha from chapter 1. As time went on, Martha knew she was burning the candle on both ends. She discussed her contract with her personnel committee, determined to cut back on her hours. The season of Advent was approaching, with additional worship activities to plan in addition to her usual ministry demands. Because she had young children, Christmas preparations and events for her family added to her customary load at home. When the deacons reminded her that they "always" offered an extra adult class in Advent, Pastor Martha knew this was beyond her capacity. She had no creative energy to initiate such a class, thought the response would be poor, and knew it would overtax her in an already-busy season.

But she knew that there were rumblings in the congregation because she had stopped attending all the evening committee meetings and had even proposed hiring someone else to work with youth. Pastor Martha was raised by parents who had high expectations that she never seemed to meet. Warding off criticism had become a way of life for her. So she gave in: after all, how hard could it be to lead a short-term book-discussion group? Pastor Martha said "yes" when every bone in her body wanted to say "no."

Martha was too busy to advertise the group widely. Attendance was as sparse as she had predicted, and because of an additional preparation, she had less energy and passion to invest in Advent and Christmas worship services. Ironically, her inability to say "no" limited her creativity and energy during Advent.

Some requests don't stir up internal resistance or disquiet. We are happy to respond, because we are fairly confident that the skills and pastoral presence we offer can make a difference. Saying "yes" to some requests feels like the fulfillment of all we hoped when we entered ministry. These requests, while taking additional time and energy, are part of what we identify as excellent ministry, and when we fulfill these requests, they leave us with more, not less, energy for ministry. What's the difference?

Suppose Martha made a conscious decision to pace herself more slowly through the Advent season? What if she encouraged her congregation to put their efforts into fewer activities for which she and the parishioners had room to prepare?

When one of the congregation's members died just before Christmas, Martha now had time to be with the family and lead them through the grief of loss and planning a memorial service during this busy time of the year. Knowing the memorial service would interfere with her home schedule, she reached out for additional help from her babysitter. She even kept an appointment with the therapist she had engaged that fall, after realizing she was giving in to congregational demands that were burning her out and not helping the congregation either.

Even though Martha's workload was busier than usual, she knew that helping the family and congregation celebrate an important life in the midst of Advent and Christmas preparations was part of what she most loved about ministry and would renew her faith as well as the faith of the family and the congregation. Because she wasn't as overstretched as she might have been, she was able to give her best to planning and conducting the memorial service.

Since some requests don't stir up internal conflict, all the more striking, then, are the times we say "yes" and we know we should say "no." How do we understand saying "yes" when we know better? This chapter looks at some of the internal reasons we may say "yes" despite knowing that we need to define our limits.

HEALTHY SELVES

Self psychology, a psychological theory of individual development based on the contributions of Heinz Kohut (1913–1981), provides one clue to understanding why we say "yes" when we want to say "no." Kohut trained as a psychoanalyst but soon came to believe that orthodox Freudian psychoanalysis was unable to resolve the problems of the patients who had come to him for help. He developed a theory of self-development through his work with those whose selfhood was fragile and who suffered from a lack of vitality.

Self psychology explains the human longing for appreciation and validation that is part of normal development. Self psychology also helps us understand that when children do not receive enough validating, appreciative responses, they are left vulnerable to perceived slights, rejections, and low self-esteem (what we mean by fragile selfhood). When we arrive in ministry with a shortage of internal resources to soothe and value ourselves, our longing for admiration and validation can drive us into the ground or lead us to make poor choices.

In the paragraph above, we've introduced two central concepts in self psychology. Validating and affirming responses, often referred to as "mirroring" responses, enable us to know more of ourselves, when our feelings, capacities, and needs are reflected authentically. "Self-soothing," the self's capacity to provide comfort and validation for ourselves, is essential to maintaining healthy self-esteem— especially when affirmation is lacking in the responses of those around us. Self psychology makes sense of our experience: when we are able to soothe ourselves over the course of life's ups and downs, we know ourselves to be more healthy than fragile.

What do we mean by the word "self"? Without getting into philosophical discussions, we use this word in its most self-evident fashion. For us, as for Kohut, the self is a unifying concept. By "self," we mean the center of ourselves, what holds us together. "Without being taught it you sense that you are a self; and . . . you also sense that your self is the nucleus, the core of who you are."[1]

Selves can be healthy or unhealthy. In Kohut's understanding, a healthy self is cohesive—that is, it can withstand challenges. A healthy self has continuity over time—that is, it provides a consistent sense of self-worth. And a healthy self is marked by vitality— that is, cohesion and consistency instill a resilience throughout life's vicissitudes. Following from this understanding, a self fails to be healthy when it is falling apart, inconsistent, or frail.

How does the healthy self develop? Like other theorists, such as English pediatrician and psychoanalyst Donald W. Winnicott (1896–1971), Kohut understood that parents aren't, and don't need to be, perfect—but they need to provide "good enough" parenting.

In optimal parenting, children have role models they can idealize and from whom they receive admiration for their gradually developing talents and skills. These two constituents of the self, having caregivers we idealize and from whom we receive admiration, form the core of healthy self-development. Good-enough parents provide adequate mirroring of who we are and who we are becoming and provide ideals to which we aspire, the foundation of our values and goals.

Optimal parenting provides an environment in which we develop healthy ambition, initiative, and assertiveness. Good-enough parents aren't perfect—and that lack of perfection is also an essential part of healthy development. Through early experiences of frustration, we learn that sometimes we must wait to have our needs met and that our caregivers won't always provide the empathic attunement (to use one of self psychology's key phrases) we need.

Through early experiences of frustration as well as our response to this frustration, we begin to experience our caregivers and ourselves as worthwhile. As we learn to trust that the caregiver will respond, however imperfectly, we form an internal self-structure that regulates our self-esteem and affirms us through the ebb and flow of support from our caregiver.

We never outgrow our need for mirroring. But as we learn we can cope with the ebb and flow of support, we learn as well that, overall, we can count on others and ourselves. Believing that we can trust others as well as ourselves enables us to develop a healthy narcissism—where the grandiosity of our infantile need for admiration is transformed into adult humor, creativity, empathy, and wisdom.

When our early experiences lead us to feel primarily mistrustful of others and to believe we do not have enough inner resources to weather the ebb and flow of life, we become vulnerable to a reactive, defensive narcissism. Our mistrust results when caregivers—

over and over again—are not dependable. When we do not experience supportive relationships and must lean on as yet inadequate internal resources, our self-esteem is easily vulnerable to slights and criticisms. We crave attention and are ashamed of our need for attention—especially if we've been taught that to seek attention is "selfish" and that to be selfish in this way is incompatible with following Jesus. We hesitate to ask for help and instead seek validation by being helpful to others. Ostensibly, being helpful in this way is compatible with the Gospel, but when it masks unconscious wounds and deficits, it can leave us open to being unconscious of our needs and acting them out in inappropriate ways.

When we are able to receive support from our primary relationships, that support becomes an internal resource to us. Based on real relationships, these internalized resources are the building blocks of healthy selves. Thus, when life becomes unpredictable or difficult, these internalized or intrapsychic relationships enable us to tolerate threats to our self-esteem, to continue to value ourselves, and to survive the ups and downs of life.

Self psychology refers to these internalized resources as "self-objects." While this label is confusing, self psychologists mean by this term the experiences of interpersonal relationships that we internalize, the aspects of relationships (objects) we use to soothe and therefore consolidate or hold together the self.

Self-objects bear some resemblance to real others and real relationships, but they are not identical with them. Our experience shapes what we take in of others and of our relationships. Self-objects are internal structures that we create out of our experiences to form reliable ways of validating and soothing ourselves.

Many of us in the helping professions were raised in families where caregivers were unable—for multiple reasons—to provide us with a secure sense of ourselves. Perhaps our parents were in unhappy marriages themselves, or our parents were themselves raised by parents who were unable to mirror our parents' talents and skills. Perhaps our caregivers were struggling with addictions or illnesses, or our families were overtaxed with illnesses among grandparents and/or siblings. The point here is not to blame but to call attention to the fact that sometimes caregivers cannot give what they do not have themselves. As children raised in such circumstances, we experience that our needs don't count and compensate (meet our needs indirectly) by listening to and attending to the needs and feelings of others. Receiving infrequent validation from a parent can mean that we spend our lives—consciously and unconsciously—looking for the parent who will affirm us, listen to us, and respond to our needs. And receiving infrequent validation from a parent may cause us to give others what we crave in the misguided hope that they will return the favor.

When we grow up needing validation, we are often unaware of the strength of that need until we bump up against the burnout or despair that comes when we find ourselves living for the acceptance and approval of others—saying "yes" when we want to say "no." What the popular press calls a "people pleaser" is the kind of person depth psychologists are describing when they point to those who have difficulty saying "no" to requests that violate our boundaries— and do so because of early unmet needs that leave us vulnerable, needing (sometimes desperately) to be liked, to be loved, to be understood, to be known, to be admired, to be valued.

Left unattended, such needs can create deep wells of vulnerability. A minister who came for counseling had formed an inappropriate relationship with a member of his congregation. As he tried to explain how this happened, he said, "I was feeling emotionally and spiritually exhausted. When I spent time with her, I felt alive again. She made me feel special. She told me how no one ever listened to her or understood her the way I did. I began to look forward to our meetings and didn't want them to end because they felt so wonderful." In the counseling process, the minister began to understand how his need for validation and attention easily led to an inappropriate relationship.

The need for attention and validation can manifest itself in less egregious but equally troubling ways, in part because of the "slippery slope" of our unaddressed need. If you visit a family in crisis at two in the morning and they tell you for weeks afterward that you saved their family and are the most wonderful minister they have ever met, then what do you have to do to get more affirmation? Setting limits and boundaries will not deliver more of that craved affirmation. The need to be liked and appreciated makes saying "no" very difficult.

Self psychology helps us understand why to our consternation we will say "yes" when we want to say anything but yes! And these concepts hold out hope—that if we can understand and work with our internal needs for mirroring and soothing, we can learn to respond in ways that are consonant with our boundaries.

LOOKING FOR LOVE IN ALL THE WRONG PLACES

The needs for affirmation and validation—to have one's feelings understood and to be admired—are normal needs that become excessive when our childhood experiences leave us vulnerable. Needs for role models to emulate, to idealize, are also normal—and problematic if left unfulfilled. When we are vulnerable in these ways, we look for members of our congregation to meet our needs rather than working to meet their needs for ministry. For example, if we look to our congregations for the validation we missed, we will have difficulty engaging our congregations as leaders, which means saying things people need—but sometimes do not want—to hear (and risking not being liked by our congregations). If we lacked a parental figure to idealize, we may find ourselves unable to say "no" to keep a valued parishioner on a pedestal—to their detriment, our own, and possibly to the detriment of our congregation.

Distinguishing when we are meeting our needs and when we are meeting the needs of our parishioners is challenging. The Roman Catholic priest, writer, and teacher Henri Nouwen (1932–1996) pointed out how our needs can make it difficult to differentiate between ourselves and others. Our needs take over, and, Nouwen wrote,

> The question no longer is, "Who is he?" but, "What can I get from him?"—and we no longer listen to what he is saying but to what we can do with what he is saying. Then the fulfillment of our unrecognized need for sympathy, friendship, popularity, success, understanding, money or a career becomes our concern, and instead of paying attention to the other person we impose ourselves upon him with intrusive curiosity. [2]

When our selfhood is fragile, in need of the shoring up from others that was in short supply in our childhoods, we may find ourselves looking to members of our congregations for self-objects, functioning to shore up our fragile self-worth. A role reversal takes place where parishioners become self-objects for the minister as opposed to the minister being the self-object for them. Many of us have watched parents becoming overly excited at Little League or soccer games and wondered why they are acting so inappropriately. Their child is functioning for them as a self-object and grounding their self-esteem. The parent's thinking is, if my child is a great athlete or great student and goes to a prestigious college, then I must have been a good parent. Roles have shifted: the parent is not there to admire the child for the child's sake, but rather the child's success is essential for the parent's self-esteem.

Our role as clergy is to serve as self-objects for our congregations—to help them through times of crisis by providing the support that strengthens their sense of self, shoring up their capacity to survive the experiences that challenge their hope. No one is able to provide such support perfectly or consistently. But like good-enough parents, good-enough clergy provide glimpses of ideals and values to admire and motivate. Our empathy and affirmation helps our parishioners know themselves as valued, loved children of God.

But if we as clergy are not able to see ourselves as valued, loved children of God, if we feel the vitality of our selfhood slipping away in the midst of personal and professional demands and have few boundaries for self-preservation, we can easily turn to parishioners for needed self-object responses. If we have few family, friends, or outside support, our reliance on our parishioners is unhealthy for us and for them.

Our roles in our families of origin—which we will discuss in chapter 3—add to our understanding of why we say "yes" when we know we need to say "no." Often clergy were the "hero" children growing up: over-responsible, taking care of the family, the peace-makers. When caregivers are impaired or unable to function— perhaps because they received inadequate care themselves—children sacrifice their needs to take care of their families. While their behavior can appear to those outside the family as heroic, what is not noticed is the cost of the validation these children receive from over-functioning in the family. When over-functioning is rewarded (for example, being praised for taking on tasks that belong to the absent or impaired caregiver), it is easy to keep over-functioning in hope of receiving more validation. Self-sacrifice and over-function-ing become a pattern that is almost addictive. Self-worth is based on what we do rather than who we are: loved children of God—a recipe for clergy burnout.

Kohut's self psychology and family-systems theory give us ways to view a problem and an unfortunate solution that has developed as a result. As Kohut observed, our lack of validation leaves us vulnerable and unconscious of our needs. But by filling a family role of hero, we sacrifice our needs in order to take care of others, receiving praise for our sacrifice. We become self-objects without a healthy self, and until we are burned out, we may never notice how empty we are beneath our over-functioning.

Rev. Amy self-referred herself for counseling. She described growing up as the oldest child in an alcoholic family: helping her parents with their finances, helping raise her siblings, and constantly living with anxiety, wondering when her parents would get in one of their no-holds-barred drunken confrontations. While her role as peacemaker and over-functioner was exhausting, and in some ways made it impossible for her to enjoy her high-school years, she received tremendous validation from both her family and extended family. She was seen as the one person who could do it all. Her sense of self was somewhat dependent on the validation she received for the hero role she played in her family of origin. In her work as a parish minister, she knew that she should be setting limits and saying "no," but at the same time, she felt invigorated by the validation she received when she over-functioned. On some level, her family-of-origin role and the validation she received from that role kept her trapped in an endless cycle of not being able to say "no." The validation was like oxygen—and it also led to burnout.

Clergy and therapists don't gravitate to the helping professions for only spiritual and altruistic reasons, as valid as these reasons are. Often, we have histories of inadequate response from our self-objects. We may have greater or lesser degrees of grandiosity, demanding that others meet our needs for admiration, acceptance, and applause. When we are starving for validating responses from our

parishioners, Jung's warning to his fellow analysts may apply equally well to clergy:

> Each profession carries its respective difficulties, and the dan-
> ger . . . [is if] the patient assumes that his analyst is the fulfill-
> ment of his dreams, that he is not an ordinary doctor but a spiri-
> tual hero, and a sort of savior. . . . [The analyst] begins to feel if
> there are saviors, well, perhaps it is just possible I am one.[3]

In what other profession are leaders called "the Reverend" and
assumed to speak for God? In what other profession do leaders tell
stories of their call to ministry that marks them as somehow special?

No one gets past an ordination committee without telling a personal story of his or her call to ministry. Calls have precedents in the
Bible: consider the prophets, who were called to less-than-glamor-
ous work but whose trust in God provided the motivation to survive
the most difficult of assignments. For clergy, too, a sense of call
may carry us through many a troubled meeting, stressful season of
the church year, too many funerals, and not enough time off. But we
need to temper our sense of call with reality: knowing ourselves
well enough to know where our selves falter, where we need shoring up, where we are vulnerable. Without such tempering, our calls
can collude with our grandiosity. We may see ourselves as special,
as being above rules, not requiring the self-care and boundaries that
protect us.

The ideas in the paragraph above—that calls to ministry need
tempering—reflect an underlying concept of self psychology known
as "narcissism." Narcissism in the popular imagination has a negative connotation, referring to persons with traits of selfishness and
self-centeredness. In self psychology, narcissism is understood differently—as an aspect of human development that can be healthy or
unhealthy. When we develop normally from children to adults, our
narcissism is tempered: we are assertive without domineering oth-

ers; we have a positive self-image without feeling superior or entitled; we have appropriate ambition without manipulating others. In other words, we express healthy narcissism, not grandiosity.

Unhealthy narcissism can develop in two directions: grandiosity, as described above, or what self psychologists call "vulnerable narcissism," in which we suffer from the opposite of grandiosity: low self-esteem, a sense of shame at the core of our being, feelings of emptiness and helplessness. In other words, healthy narcissism is the center of a continuum, and unhealthy narcissism is found on either end of the continuum as grandiosity or vulnerability.

In chapter 1, we cited the statistic that more men perpetrate clergy sexual misconduct and more women are the victim/survivors of CSM. Perhaps Kohut and the self psychologists offer one possible explanation: that unhealthy narcissism in men is more likely to be of the grandiose variety, expressed through domineering behaviors, superior and entitled attitudes. As Valerie Saiving, one of the founding voices of feminist theology, notes, theology has defined "pride" and domination as a sin.[4] But pride and domination may be more problematic for men than for women, whose very underdevelopment of selfhood could be understood as a sin. Sheryl Sandberg, the COO of Facebook, documents the multitude of ways in which women still have a long way to go to develop themselves in the world of work and leadership.[5]

Many of us in the helping professions—from clergy to therapists (and in the case of the coauthors, both clergy and therapists)—turned to those professions to heal early wounds in our developing selves. In this chapter, we've explored the wounds of not receiving needed validation or the mirroring that enables us to soothe ourselves—foundations for healthy selfhood. We've also seen how a precocious, unconscious family role may spur us into levels of overfunctioning that lead to burnout and boundary problems. Perhaps we chose our respective professions knowing our need for healing. Unable to ask for help directly, we approached our needs indirectly, by learning to help others. But our help will fall short if we don't take the time to get to know our strengths and resources as well as our wounds, taking care not to project our needs onto those who need us.

Henri Nouwen understood that if we are able to understand and address our own wounds, we will have a deeper capacity to help others in their healing process. Nouwen proclaims good news for the wounded healer:

> A deep understanding of his own pain makes it possible for him to convert his weakness into strength and to offer his own experience as a source of healing to those who are often lost in the darkness of their own misunderstood sufferings.[6]

PRACTICE

1. Get to know your hot buttons. Identify a time in your ministry when you became furious with some issue or person. What was going on within you? Can you identify any needs within yourself that were unmet—for example, needs for admiration, recognition, and comfort?
2. Get to know your vulnerabilities. Think of some instances in your life when you felt yourself in danger of disintegrating or falling apart, when you felt particularly vulnerable or weak. Describe those situations as fully as you can, especially exploring your inner needs and the responses (or lack of responses) from people around you.
3. Get to know your strengths. Think of a time when you could have fallen apart because of a load of stress or difficult interactions. What did you need? How were your needs being met? What kept you from falling apart?

4. Reflect on your spiritual resources. Identify a practice that helps you soothe yourself. For example, prayer for some is a way to connect with God as comforter, as the one to whom you belong, as the one whose recognition forms you. After you have identified a self-soothing ritual, practice it daily.

3

SETTING BOUNDARIES IN ANXIOUS CONGREGATIONAL SYSTEMS

At a congregational meeting in a large, suburban congregation struggling with multiple problems, a board member stood up to speak about what he considered the source of the congregation's problems. He said with great authority, "The problem with our minister is that he does not understand that his job is to be available 24/7."

The board member went on to list a number of ways that the minister in question had set boundaries around his time. He listed in painful detail how their minister had set several nights to be family nights and how his wife did not go to all the women's luncheons due to her own work schedule. He then reminded the congregation that their former minister, who had served the congregation for thirty-six years, told people to call him anytime and even donated all the honorariums from weddings and funerals back to the church. Sadly, no one from the congregation supported the current minister and his attempt to set healthy boundaries around his time. Nor did anyone challenge the accuracy of the board member's statements or offer any type of rebuttal. The minister, who had attempted to set boundaries, had now become the focus of all that was wrong with the congregation.

While healthy boundaries are essential for effective ministry, this example underscores how costly it can be to set boundaries without congregational support. This is especially true for congregations that are in decline and therefore anxious about the future. Such congregations hope desperately that their ministers' efforts will turn the congregation around. Congregational anxiety and heightened expectations can create a very difficult context in which to set boundaries even for the most well-intentioned clergy. While not all congregations are anxiety driven, setting boundaries in those congregations that are struggling can prove to be extraordinarily challenging. In early boundary-awareness trainings, congregational resistance to boundaries was not addressed, but the topic has come up in every boundary-awareness training we have provided since 1995. Usually halfway through the training, someone asks: "Why is this not being taught in my congregation? My congregation pushes back when I set a boundary."

Even if clergy can understand the need for boundaries and work through their needs for validation and to be liked, as explained in the previous chapter, they are frequently trying to set boundaries in anxious church systems with high expectations. The higher the congregational anxiety, the more difficult it is to set limits, particularly for clergy in small congregations. In small-church contexts, clergy are expected to be generalists, successful at everything. If they try to set limits, focusing their efforts on a few specific pastoral activities, such as preaching and pastoral care, congregational resistance can be significant.

Of course, less anxious congregations exist. Boards and personnel committees, encouraged by denominational leaders, can learn to support and encourage clergy in setting personal and professional limits. But systems theory reminds us that thinking about problems only in terms of individuals without understanding the context in which they work will never provide an adequate picture of the unique struggles individual clergy encounter in their particular work systems. This chapter helps readers better understand congregations as a system and the multiple factors that can interfere with clergies and congregations understanding and appreciating appropriate boundaries. This understanding is essential to effect change. Practical suggestions on how to work with congregations to set appropriate boundary expectations are offered in more detail in chapter 5.

While systems theory is often identified with family therapy, general systems theory encompasses a way of seeing and thinking that is very different from traditional linear thinking. While family systems theory is obviously focused on family dynamics, general systems theory can be applied to much larger systems, such as congregations. Linear thinking assumes that A causes B, and any problem in B must be the result of A. In contrast, systems theory assumes that A and B are constantly influencing each other.

Systems theory changes the way we conceptualize problems. For example, when a congregation is struggling, members often search for a simple cause. "Our problems are because our minister doesn't reach out to the community," or "If we could just get a new choir director, everything would be all right." It is difficult for members of a congregation to look at their problem in context and recognize that, in fact, there is no one cause but rather that a number of factors—such as a changing community, aging congregation, poor communication by the board—are interacting.

Many congregations have difficulty understanding the systemic nature of their problems. For example, members of First Baptist Church state that they do not trust their minister and that their problems are related to the need for a new minister. However, in examining the congregation through systems theory, a different picture emerges. The personnel committee has been in conflict with the minister but does not speak to the administrative board about the problem. The committee's information has come largely from a few disgruntled members and the church secretary. The administrative board is aware of some of the issues but does not have regular conversations with the personnel committee. Meanwhile a "parking lot committee" has formed, and it has its own version of the problem and circulates its theories about the cause of the problem by email with another subset of the congregation. It is clear that First Baptist does have a problem with trust; it is not so clear that the problem is the minister. Rather, the way the system communicates has created a context where trust will be difficult to establish.

Systems theory, in contrast to linear thinking, is concerned with understanding the relationship of the whole with its interacting parts, and the interaction of the whole with the larger environment.[1] Systems theory helps us understand people in the context of the environment in which they live and work and tries to explore all problems in a larger context. First Baptist is an example of the contextual nature of the problem.

Not surprisingly, when we think systemically, our emphasis shifts from the intrapersonal to the interpersonal. Systems theory examines the congregation's role along with other factors in the development of problems and how the congregational system can maintain and even exacerbate those problems in addition to other system factors such as historical issues and community issues. In the case of First Baptist, the poor communication between the board and committees, as well as the underground nature of communication, has created a context that makes problems difficult to resolve. So in a discussion of boundary problems, systems theory invites us to consider the contribution of the congregational system to the problem and how the congregation's issues may even increase the prevalence of boundary problems and burnout. Systems theory also offers an explanation for how healthy systems work and how they can even build on their strengths. In any discussion of boundary issues, the system within which individuals act may make boundary setting more complicated, or it may create a context where boundaries are supported and ministry thrives.

Urie Bronfenbrenner,[2] one of the pioneers of general systems theory, expanded the concept of a system to include multiple systems. His theory suggested that systems are embedded within systems and that in the end the individual does not have nearly as much agency as most of us would like to believe. In his theory of child development, Bronfenbrenner explains that the child is part of a family system, which in turn is part of an extended-family system, which is embedded in other systems (such as schools and churches), all of which in turn are part of a larger social system. When we visualize these interconnected systems, we become clear that helping the child is impossible without addressing the systems in which the child is embedded. This model was the impetus for the creation of Head Start and other social-service programs that aim to impact individuals through systemic interventions.

Professionals influenced by Bronfenbrenner recognized that the most effective way to help a child was to work not only with the child but also to attempt to change the systems that the child was part of—for example, to work both with the child's family as well as the school that the child attends. When the family and school work together to create common goals and plans for the child, the child's behavior or academic performance often improves. Suppose Joey is having angry outbursts in school. Teaching him anger-management techniques will most likely not be helpful. Seeing Joey together with his family reveals, however, that his parents constantly fight in front of him and that tension permeates the family, in part because Joey's father has been out of work for six months and is feeling very anxious and frustrated. When Joey's parents can be helped to better manage both their anxiety and conflict, and then can learn appropriate ways to set clear boundaries with Joey, his angry outbursts may begin to change. When the parents can meet with teachers and they can all agree to use a common strategy when Joey becomes angry, Joey's outbursts will most likely decrease as a result of getting the same message from both parents and teachers. As the communication between parents and teachers increases, Joey's behavior will continue to improve. While it is important for Joey's behavior to change, and he will certainly be given guidance for shifting his behavior, it is difficult for the change to occur unless the systems around Joey also change.

Bronfenbrenner's theory is useful in understanding the dilemmas many clergy face. Like Joey and his family, they are embedded in multiple contexts including a congregation, which, if it is embedded in the larger context of mainline Christianity, is in a system in decline. As congregations fear for their future in the midst of an aging and declining membership, they often become more anxious. And the mainline Christian church itself is embedded in a larger cultural system where younger people, especially in certain parts of the country, do not view institutional religion favorably. Using Bronfenbrenner's theory helps put the problem of clergy in perspective. Too often, congregations expect that the many problems they are encountering can be fixed by a creative, energetic minister, without factoring in the larger cultural context. This obviously puts a lot of pressure on individual clergy and may make it even more difficult for them to set boundaries.

As an example, First United Methodist Church was once a thriving dynamic parish. Its large sanctuary could hold eight hundred people, a new education wing had been added in its prime to accommodate a large church school, and in its golden years, both were packed. However, over the past thirty years, two of the primary employers in the community have shut down their operations, increasing unemployment and encouraging people to move away to find employment elsewhere. Now on a Sunday morning, there are often about seventy people sitting in a large sanctuary, and most are over the age of sixty-five. The Sunday school has a handful of kids, and the choir has declined to a few faithful singers. The board is afraid the congregation will not be able to afford both a full-time minister and a part-time organist, and board members worry about how they will raise the money to keep up their old building, which now needs a roof and a number of other repairs. They have decided the congregation will worship in the fellowship hall during the winter, so they do not have to pay to heat the sanctuary. They are desperately trying to rent office space in their educational wing to outside organizations to help ends meet. They have spent down much of the congregation's endowment, and weekly giving covers only part of their budget. Recently, when the finance committee of the board met, anxiety escalated. The finance committee now predicts that the endowment will be exhausted in seven years, at which time the church may not be able to stay open. Not surprisingly, these discussions spike everyone's anxiety even higher. Board and committee meetings are increasingly filled with tension, and members are becoming more reactive. Meanwhile, a large evangelical church a mile away is flourishing, drawing many young people, perhaps thanks to its contemporary worship style and large youth group.

The solution of the board members was to hope the right minister would turn the church around. They were excited when Pastor Joann arrived as their minister. She was young, had great energy, and seemed to have good ideas. However, after she had been their leader for three years, not much had changed, at least according to the board. Despite some creative changes to worship and excellent pastoral care, neither the attendance nor giving had increased much. People were becoming more critical, and Joann was becoming anxious. She was constantly reminded that money was tight and that attendance was not increasing, despite her innovations and long workweeks. She began to have problems sleeping and sometimes woke in the middle of the night wondering what was going to happen.

Joann knows that despite the criticism and increasing anxiety, she needs to take some time off for study leave. She has been working long hours and has neglected physical exercise as well as her spiritual disciplines. She wants to take a week off to attend a national preaching conference and connect with some old seminary friends, but when she mentions this to parishioners, people become negative and point to all the problems in the church, not to mention reminding her of the congregation's tight budget. Her husband is worried and sees what the constant stress and pressure is doing to Joann and does not know what to do. From a boundary perspective, Joann knows she needs to say "no" to some things, take some time to regroup and reenergize. But setting boundaries in the context of First United Methodist will prove very difficult. She will need to find ways to inoculate herself from taking on the congregation's anxiety, maintaining a commitment to taking care of herself relationally, spiritually, and physically while continuing to honor her call to ministry at First United Methodist. Important first steps will include enlisting the support of the congregation's personnel committee for maintaining self-care, educating the congregation about the overlapping anxieties that are impacting their ministry, and helping them understand healthy and unhealthy responses to anxiety and to identify healthy responses for their congregation's life and ministry.

Reverend Joann and First United Methodist Church illustrate the problem of an individual trying to set boundaries in the midst of significant systemic anxiety. First United Methodist is anxious due to declining and aging membership and declining finances, in the midst of a community struggling with unemployment. Joann is anxious as a result of the pressure she feels to try to turn this congregation around. In chapter 5 we will explore some practical steps that Joann (and all clergy in similar situations) can take to address these very complicated issues around anxiety. As we will explore in chapter 5, anxiety is highly contagious, and therefore an important boundary for clergy in Joann's situation will be to find ways of setting internal boundaries as a kind of inoculation against infection with congregational anxiety so that their own vision is sustained.

THE CONTRIBUTIONS OF MURRAY BOWEN

Murray Bowen's theory[3] is extremely helpful in exploring in more depth the challenges of boundary setting and the potential for burnout. Many clergy are indirectly aware of the work of Murray Bowen due to the many authors who have popularized his theory, including the late Edwin Friedman and Ron Richardson, to name a few.[4] Bowen's comprehensive theory greatly enhances our understanding of boundaries and burnout. Central to Bowen's theory are eight

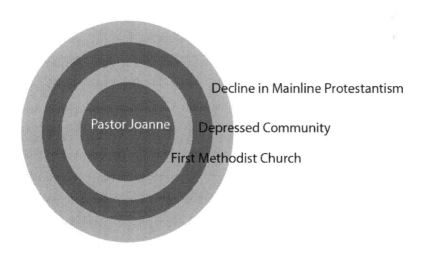

Figure 3.1.

basic concepts, which include: the family emotional system, multi-generational transmission, triangles, emotional cutoff, sibling position, differentiation of self, family projection process, and societal emotional system. Because a number of these concepts are particularly relevant to congregational systems, they are elaborated in what follows.

CHURCH AS AN EMOTIONAL SYSTEM

Central to Bowen's theory is his understanding of the family as an emotional system that operates according to general systems theory. When systems theory asserts that the sum is always greater than the parts, it explains our experience that a system has a life of its own and is bigger and more complicated than the individual people in the system. To better understand this theory, try to visualize your frequent fight or argument with a significant other in your life (partner, child, family member, or friend). Pretend that your fight was caught on camera without you being aware of it. In watching the film of your argument in stop action, you would see how the argument begins and escalates, how emotion intensifies, how both people become more emotionally reactive, and finally how the argument ends. For many of us, this film would not be flattering. When we are especially anxious, stressed, or tired, we become more reactive, and our capacity for creative thinking or problem solving is diminished.

Neuroscientists call this phenomenon an "amygdala hijack." High anxiety makes it difficult to utilize the prefrontal cortex, and too often the more primitive part of the brain, the amygdala, takes over. The amygdala will often default to fight or flight or even freeze. During these times, our bodies are fueled by adrenaline, and we are hardly at our best. While we may want to believe that we are rational people, the film view of our argument shows that we are driven by emotion, not rationality. We may begin the argument attempting to not get "hooked" or become reactive, but in the end, the dance of emotional reactivity is set in motion.

Bowen suggested that as families become more anxious and overwhelmed, an emotional process takes place that may start with a couple but might also pull in other members of the family. For example, during times of significant tension or anxiety, each spouse may lose self-awareness and blame the other for all the problems. Or one spouse may over-function to help contain the anxiety during a family crisis but then run the risk of becoming symptomatic. The anxiety spills over when a woman who overcompensates for her husband's drinking and resultant problems at work becomes highly involved with her children's school projects and winds up diag-nosed with depression. Other couples may project their anxiety onto one of the children. As a child acts out in school, the couple's anxiety may lessen, as they form more of a partnership to solve their child's problem. All of these are examples of the family acting as an emotional system: an interdependent emotional unit in which family members function in reciprocal relationship to one another.[5]

This concept of emotional system extends beyond families to congregations. Like families, congregational emotional process is rarely conscious and is often not understood. First Presbyterian Church, for example, was in crisis. Known for its social-justice stance, strong preaching, wonderful music program, and powerful history, the congregation has now begun to struggle. Their last min-ister, after almost thirty years of ministry characterized by a formal and authoritative style, retired due to health concerns and a number of rumors about misconduct. Following a two-year interim and a long nationwide search, their new minister, Reverend Alan, has been serving for three and a half years, bringing a style different from the congregation's past experience with pastoral leadership.

Despite its reputation as the strongest church in the community, attendance dropped, pledges were down, and anxiety was up. The congregation was aging, many members retired to a warmer climate, and younger families were not replacing lost members. As the anxiety increased, morale decreased. The board was split. One group was convinced they called the wrong minister. Another faction believed that they had never dealt with some of the issues surrounding their last minister, including allegations of alcoholism and possible sexual misconduct and a sense that he had coasted for the last five years of his ministry. The choir began to talk after practice about how they missed the style of music they used to sing before their new minister changed some of the music. Others believed, though, that they would need to make even more major changes in their programming and worship style to attract younger members. A group of wealthy older members stopped attending, held private meetings in one of their homes, and decided together to stop paying their pledges. Meanwhile, the personnel committee began a new evaluation process of their new minister without working with the board. In addition, Pastor Alan was considering updating his résumé, believing that he made a mistake coming to First Presbyterian.

In Bowen's theory, the congregational emotional system had become infected with anxiety. Communication had gone underground, groups were not talking directly to each other, and each group was projecting its anxiety on another group or issue. Since each group is projecting the anxiety onto another group or person, and not communicating directly, it will be difficult for anyone in this congregational emotional system to get a clear picture of the problem.

On a much simpler level, think about board meetings or committee meetings that become reactive when a controversial topic comes up. Too often as emotions build, members begin to get reactive, and an emotional pattern emerges that leaves everyone frustrated and confused about what happened or how the discussion got so tense. By the end of the meeting, the emotional process makes resolving the issue impossible, and in some cases, group members cannot even get clear on what the real issue is.

Both examples illustrate Bowen's understanding of the emotional system. Clergy leaders are connected to parishioners, committees, and boards, which form networks of relationships or "families." Emotional processes form between these networks and can make leadership extremely challenging. When congregational systems become anxious, they deal with the anxiety in a variety of ways. We'll review in more detail projection, scapegoating, triangles, and multi-generational transmission.

FAMILY PROJECTION PROCESS

Projection is one of the ways the emotional system handles anxiety. Bowen argues that as families become more anxious, they often project the anxiety onto one of their children, helping the parents feel less anxious. For example, if a couple's marriage is in crisis and they have little to talk about, projecting a problem onto one of their children will give them a common problem to focus on, which will at least temporarily lower their anxiety and give them an issue in common. In the same way, anxious congregations like First Presbyterian project their anxiety onto a group, person, or cause. Projection initially lowers anxiety because it offers a simple solution to the problem.

Following a consultation with a large suburban congregation, after I (David) had attempted to frame the larger systems issues, the board chair said with great authority, "Our problem is simple: we need a new minister who is a leader. Why are we talking about these other issues?" He had no interest in the congregation's lack of trust, poor communication, committees that did not talk to each other, and informal committees that met in the parking lot and emailed their concerns to other members. He insisted, "If we had a real leader, these issues would disappear."

SCAPEGOATING

One powerful type of projection is scapegoating. The Old Testament concept of scapegoating described in the book of Leviticus evokes the tradition of bringing two male goats before the people. The High Priest slaughtered one goat as a sacrifice for the people. The other goat had a different function. The High Priest symbolically placed the sins of the people upon the second goat and sent it out into the wilderness as a sign of their sins being carried away.

Family systems theory often uses the concept of a scapegoat to illustrate the way that some families function, focusing on one of their children as *the* problem in the family. "We would be a healthy family if Joan would just stop getting in so much trouble. She causes us so much stress." That formulation of the problem blocks the family from exploring other causes of family stress and suggests a simplistic explanation of their problems as a family. While Joan may in fact be contributing significant stress to the family, there is likely much more going on in the family, with some family issues contributing to Joan's acting out. But it is simpler—and decreases anxiety—if the family blames Joan as the scapegoat for all the family problems.

In congregational life, too often clergy become the scapegoat for their congregations. Most congregations are concerned about growth, finance, and attracting younger families. They often have high expectations of their minister, and so when growth does not occur, congregations blame the minister, who functions as the scapegoat for the congregational problem. Other factors, such as an aging congregation that has been in decline for the last twenty years, as well as a changing community, are not factored in. The anxiety in this congregation all becomes focused on the minister—a simple target for all the congregation's problems. It is far more complicated to look at a complex array of issues in a congregation, and so much easier to look for a single cause. Obviously, clergy are not the only persons scapegoated in congregations. However, clergy are only too aware of how quickly they can be scapegoated and so as a result find it difficult to set boundaries so as not to become the scapegoat for the systemic problems of the congregation.

TRIANGLES AND ANXIETY

Another key Bowen concept is triangles. Dyads can be difficult to maintain in the midst of anxiety. When anxiety increases, the dyad frequently draws in a third person to temporarily stabilize the dyadic relationship. Consider our previous example in which a couple's relationship becomes too anxious, so a third person, often one of their children, is pulled in. When that child acts out in school, the couple's relationship is stabilized temporarily as the couple works together to help solve their child's problem. Or consider the plight of two siblings attending a family reunion that they have dreaded attending. Both are somewhat anxious about being there and so begin to talk together about their youngest sibling that didn't come to the reunion. As they talk about all of their sibling's problems with alcohol and maintaining employment, their own anxiety about attending the reunion is lowered, and they have achieved a temporary sense of artificial intimacy. They are closer to each other at the expense of their sibling. Triangles in congregational settings are all too familiar. "Pastor, I want to tell you about what the Smith family

is going through so you can pray for them and help them. Please
don't tell them I told you about their son's legal problems." The
minister is now in an uncomfortable triangle. He has received information he cannot use, while the person telling him the secret is
trying to achieve greater closeness by telling a secret. Triangles are
a significant part of congregational life. A member of the personnel
committee has lunch with Pastor Jeanne, who has been at St. Ste-
phens for eight months. Over lunch, this board member begins to
explain to Pastor Jeanne that several members of the board are
becoming very critical of her preaching but then refuses to disclose
which members are critical. He states he is very worried about Pastor Jeanne and wants to be helpful and suggests they meet for lunch
to make plans on what to do about these unnamed board members.

The men's prayer group of the Church of the Good Shepherd talk
frequently to Dan, their associate minister, about how ineffective
the senior minister is and how they wish Dan had more authority in
the congregation and wish he would preach more frequently. Dan
appreciates their trust in him, as well as the affirmation that he
receives from this group. At the same time, he is increasingly anxious about his relationship with his colleague Stan, the senior minister, which is becoming increasingly tense.

A struggling Lutheran church decides that starting an alternative,
contemporary worship service before their regular service would be
a way to attract younger members. Several board members and their
minister researched the structure of such a service and visited a
number of congregations to experience this worship style. The
board voted to move this concept forward and provided some financial resources to help it start. The new service was launched with
some success. However, a number of members were bothered by
this change and were convinced it was too much of a departure from
their regular traditional liturgy. They organized an informal group
and began sharing their concerns with other members about how

their church was changing. A number of these disgruntled members began writing letters to the board suggesting that the board was too influenced by their young minister. The board became extremely anxious and decided to call a congregational meeting. In preparation for the meeting, those who were against the new service recruited inactive members to attend the meeting to support their cause. The level of anxiety had now increased significantly due to the triangles, and many people lost track of the actual issue as a result of being brought into the emotional triangles. Too often in a conflicted congregation, members who have been recruited into triangles do not even know what the real issues are. If clergy are not firm, setting clear boundaries when members attempt to pull them into triangles, they may find themselves more anxious and ineffective. The potential for becoming triangled by members, boards, and committees is enormous. As a result, it becomes important for clergy to work with their boards and committees to address clear ground rules for communication and help the boards accept this as a way of functioning. This would include ground rules for addressing problems directly, clear guidelines for not creating triangles by talking with others outside the official meetings about what the board is addressing, and practicing open communication. It can be very helpful to keep these ground rules posted during meetings. Some congregations with multiple staff have drafted church covenants that state that if a member tries to talk to one staff member about another, the staff member will ask the person to go with him to talk directly to the other staff person, thereby staying out of a potential triangle. Given the power of this issue, it is important that triangles and the need for direct communication, along with ground rules for congregational life, be discussed regularly.

MULTIGENERATIONAL TRANSMISSION

Another key Bowen principle is that of multigenerational transmission. Bowen suggests that looking at a family over three or four generations will reveal key patterns, such as how conflict is processed, the rules for intimacy, patterns of addiction and abuse, gender roles, and how anxiety is handled. Seeing only a one-generational picture of an individual is to see the individual out of context. Looking at a person in the context of a three- or four-generational genogram or family map presents a much different picture.

Congregations also have histories that are important to understand. Many clergy have followed a long-term, beloved pastor and have been informed of how their predecessor worked seven days a week and was always available. That is difficult enough. However, many congregations also have secrets and unresolved conflicts that can easily become projected onto their new minister. When Pastor Larry arrived at First United Church, he was warmly welcomed. The first year went well, and people were pleased with his leadership and commented positively on his sermons. However, in his second year, Pastor Larry began to set several boundaries, including reshaping the job description of the church secretary, as well as posting his office hours and when he would be available for pastoral care. While these initial boundaries seemed proactive and positive, several people commented on his lack of availability when they called. Communication problems escalated when several triangles formed in the proverbial parking lot. As word traveled indirectly, several parishioners began to talk about not trusting Pastor Larry and wondering what he was doing when he was not in the office. Over the next year, more people began to talk about whether they could trust him. Larry was confused by what was happening and felt that, no matter how he explained himself, a number of people were still talking about how they didn't trust him.

What Pastor Larry did not know was that, two ministers ago, there had been a significant boundary violation involving sexual misconduct that was never processed openly. The offending minister left suddenly, and the misconduct was never discussed in any formal or direct way. Some people knew and talked to their friends about the situation, but the congregation as a whole never processed what happened. Some members were never let in on the secret. Not surprisingly, the minister who preceded Pastor Larry only lasted two years before he left, not knowing why no one seemed to trust his leadership. Bowen's concept of multigenerational transmission explains how a congregation's history can lead to significant projection on, and scapegoating of, the current minister, creating an impossible situation for pastoral self-care and boundaries. When joining a church system, a new minister has an opportunity to ask non-threatening questions about his or her predecessors and what their leadership style was, simple questions like: "Could you tell me what you most valued in the last minister?" "What were the criticisms?" "How would you describe the leadership styles of the last three ministers?" "What are the controversial issues in this congregation?" Questions designed to learn the congregation's history are a place to start an important task of the first year or two of a new call: discerning as much as possible about the congregation's communication patterns, history of over-functioning and under-functioning between clergy and lay, projection and scapegoating of the pastor, and so on.

CHRONIC ANXIETY

While triangles, scapegoating, and projection are always happening in any emotional system, they are heightened during times of increased anxiety. If a family is going through a time of prolonged anxiety and stress, symptoms will appear. In the case of a family, these symptoms may emerge as heightened marital conflict where each spouse externalizes his or her anxiety into the marital relationship and each focuses on what is wrong with the other, losing self-focus. Congregations also exhibit increased symptoms when anxiety increases. Bowen's axiom is: the greater the level of anxiety, the more primitive the functioning of members.

There are two types of anxiety: acute and chronic. Acute anxiety is a response to a particular crisis. Typically an acute crisis (job loss, health crisis, divorce) creates a spike of anxiety that is significant but relatively short-lived. If the individual (or family) is healthy and receives good support, he or she typically will recover over time, returning to his or her baseline of health. Chronic anxiety, however, is different. Chronic anxiety results from a cluster of stressors over such a lengthy period of time that the healthy baseline disappears. Over time, everyday anxiety becomes normal, even though it might be impacting both physical health (blood pressure, gastrointestinal problems, headaches, etc.) and mental health (depression, addiction, etc.). The state of chronic anxiety becomes the baseline.

In times of chronic anxiety, functioning becomes more reactive and primitive. Self-focus and self-awareness decrease, projection and blame increase, and emotional reactivity also increases.

During periods of chronic anxiety in a marriage, one spouse may give up more self in a reactive effort to stabilize the marriage or family and decrease the anxiety, over-functioning in an attempt to shore up the relationship. Consider what happens in an alcoholic family: the non-drinking spouse tries to manage the problem drinker's life. She or he hides the alcohol, calls the workplace with excuses, and takes on most of the responsibility for the children. Over-functioning is a response driven by chronic anxiety. However, over time, the spouse that gives up more self as an anxious response to the crisis in the family becomes symptomatic with either mental-health or physical-health issues. So even if the alcoholic eventually gets help, the partner often ends up symptomatic and depressed. In much the same way, the spouse of a person with a terminal illness over-functions by necessity, giving up much self to care for the other. After the funeral, however, they are often left depressed, depleted, and exhausted in a way that goes beyond normal grief. And of course, during these times of chronic anxiety, one does not choose a response rationally but rather responds reactively, driven by an attempt to create stability.

In some families, during these times of chronic anxiety, the anxiety is projected onto one of the children. The projection can be that of idealization (the perfect child) or the opposite (the problem child). Either projection shifts a great deal of anxiety onto the child, who can easily become symptomatic, not surprisingly, often presenting with anxiety disorders. When this happens, the anxiety in the family system is temporarily decreased, and the family can put all their focus on the child—thereby creating a new homeostasis.

THE PARISH FAMILY AND CHRONIC ANXIETY

If reactive patterns happen so easily in a nuclear family, imagine how powerfully reactivity occurs in a church family. Many congregations in mainline Christianity are dealing with chronic anxiety and fear for their very survival. At the same time, they are not even aware that their reactivity is driven by chronic anxiety. They forget to look at the larger crisis in the mainline church or in their communities and default to projecting their anxiety onto something more concrete. Bowen theorizes that anxiety must be "bound" somewhere. Like a nuclear family, there are a number of possibilities within a parish on which to project the anxiety: the minister is the most obvious victim.

In the end, understanding how parish systems respond to chronic anxiety offers us another way to view the complexity of setting boundaries. While clergy can go through endless boundary-awareness training and prepare to set healthy boundaries, they are in the end attempting to do so in the midst of anxious parish systems that may resent those boundaries and work even work harder to block healthy boundaries from being implemented. Systems theory stops us from blaming the parish or the minister as the "bad guy" in an anxious system looking for a simple fix. When anxiety increases, there is usually a commensurate increase in projection, triangles, and scapegoating, all of which make boundary setting difficult to achieve. Learning to set clear ground rules for communicating openly, and practicing these rules relentlessly, is an essential response in an anxious system.

DIFFERENTIATION

We can easily feel overwhelmed when we realize how the emotional system operates in times of intense anxiety. Bowen's concept of differentiation of self offers hope. Differentiation of self is the ability to contain our reactivity in the midst of anxiety, not become emotionally reactive, and stay connected to others in the midst of anxious times. Differentiation is "the ability to be in emotional contact with others yet still autonomous in one's emotional functioning."[6] It is the ability to maintain emotional objectivity while in the midst of an emotional system in turmoil. Too often people misunderstand this concept as a move toward being cutoff or independent. For example, someone may state their family is "crazy" and so as a result have little or nothing to do with them except during holidays and even then attempt to keep the conversation very much on the surface. For Bowen, avoidance is not differentiation, but instead, an emotional cutoff. True differentiation is the ability to go home, not become emotionally reactive, and attempt to maintain a one-to-one relationship with key members of the family.

In Bowen-based therapy, the focus is on spending more time going home, for the purpose of building relationships, and learning to contain personal reactivity. Bowen-based therapy does not stop with learning to talk about our "dysfunctional families" with our therapists, which can be another type of triangle, but challenges clients to figure out how to go home and be with our families in a nonreactive way.

In a similar way, clergy must learn to nonreactively stay in relationship with a variety of people and groups in their congregations while staying true to themselves while doing it. Trying to keep everyone happy is not differentiation nor is avoiding or cutting off from unpleasant people. Differentiation is the ability to lead, set clear boundaries, say "no" when necessary, while at the same time building intimate relationships—even with those with whom we disagree. It is the ability to be clear about one's gifts and abilities and set priorities to implement those gifts in a way that moves toward pastoral excellence. Trying to be all things to all people while keeping everyone happy is the path to mediocrity and the antithesis of differentiation.

For clergy to be able to set boundaries effectively and move toward more creative ministry, they must develop significant differentiation levels. Understanding the congregation as an anxious, emotional system and how that emotional system impacts leadership is a necessary first step in moving toward self-differentiation. How to begin moving toward increased levels of differentiated leadership will be addressed in chapter 5.

PRACTICE

1. Identify the issues that are contributing to anxiety in your congregation and community and whether the anxiety is acute or chronic.

2. Identify some of the (most likely) unconscious ways the congregation responds:

   - Who do they scapegoat?
   - What cutoffs are happening?
   - What triangles have been created to cope with the anxiety and stabilize the emotional system?

3. Identify one professional or personal situation and explore in depth:

   - What issues are you most anxious about?
   - Where do you notice yourself becoming most emotional and reactive?
   - Are there situations and people you've scapegoated?
   - Who have you pulled into triangles to decrease your anxiety?
   - Who are you avoiding or cutting off?

4. What would it be like for you to stop scapegoating? How would you do that? How could you reach out to connect with those who are cut off? How could you stop engaging in triangles?

5. What helps you contain reactive behavior? Recalling chapter 2, what self-soothing practices might help you?

4

WHEN THE SELF AND
SYSTEM COLLIDE

As we observed in chapter 1, too often books and workshops on boundaries or burnout focus either on the self of the minister or on the complexities of navigating the congregational system. Our premise is that boundary and burnout problems result from interactions between the minister and the congregational system. In this interactional approach, we focus not simply on the individual issues of the minister or the anxiety-driven issues within the congregation but rather on how the minister defines himself or herself within the congregational system and how the system responds.

These two variables function in a reciprocal relationship and can form a complicated feedback loop. Ministers who are not as dependent on validation from congregants, and who are better at both containing their own anxiety and relating to key people, are more likely to successfully set appropriate boundaries. And the more enlightened and understanding the congregation, the greater the odds of those boundaries resulting in healthy and creative ministry since boundaries create room without distraction to focus on mission.

While these two approaches—focusing on the clergy's self or on the congregational system—may seem like different paradigms, in reality they work well together. Self psychology views internal experience through the subjective lens of the self, while Bowenian approaches view the self through a systemic lens. Rather than being contradictory, these two approaches are simply different lenses through which to view the problems clergy encounter. Used together, they help us understand how the intrapsychic and subjective experience of clergy interact with the complex systems in the congregations they serve.

Pastor Steve provided a painful example of the interaction effect between his intrapsychic needs, unresolved systemic issues from his family of origin, and systemic issues in the congregation he served. Pastor Steve grew up in a difficult alcoholic family. He was the oldest of four children and provided his mother's greatest support in dealing with his alcoholic father, who sometimes flew into a rage after drinking. Steve took on the role of the protector and hero in the family. He was the model student and athlete who never got into trouble and was admired by both his teachers and coaches and frequently pointed to as a role model. He tried in vain to keep everything calm at home in the hopes that his father would stop drinking or at least not get violent. He attempted to keep discussions at the dinner table nonconfrontational and tried to help his mother take care of his siblings. Without consciously choosing to do so, he became hyper-vigilant in his attempt to keep things peaceful. He described to his therapist always being on alert and mildly anxious as he attempted to prevent possible catastrophes. He believed that relaxing would increase the possibility that he would miss something, with disastrous consequences. His mother confided all of her anxieties and frustrations about his father to Steve, almost putting him in the position of a pseudo-spouse. Steve played multiple roles in the family: hero, perfect son, peacemaker, and marriage counselor. He received constant mirroring and validation from his mother and teachers for being the perfect child and was seen as more of an adult then a child. He jokingly claimed that he never had a childhood since he was so busy parenting his parents. Unfortunately, much of his self-esteem was based on the praise he received for his role in the family.

When Steve went to seminary, his mother and extended family were thrilled, and of course he excelled, becoming a leader among his classmates. He helped out as a student assistant in a large congregation during his final year of seminary and was loved by the congregation. After finishing seminary and getting married, Steve began his first full-time call serving a very difficult congregation. The previous minister had ended his tenure badly, with a number of allegations about questionable ethical practices. Some of the congregation loved the former pastor and believed he was unfairly pushed out, while another faction thought the judicatory should have taken disciplinary actions against him. A powerful split was emerging in the congregation, with some angry with the former minister and others singing his praises. Members of the two factions were not talking to each other, and their positions had become more and more rigid and polarized. The level of anxiety was palpable and manifested in a number of ways, including people stopping their contributions and a number of families dropping out of the church. This was the context of Steve's ministry.

Without realizing it, Pastor Steve had reentered his family of origin. The emotional climate of the congregation was familiar to Steve and replicated much of how he felt growing up. He found himself in his familiar roles of peacemaker, confidant to a number of unhappy congregants, and being recruited into numerous triangles—just as he had been in his family of origin. Because being liked and validated was important to Pastor Steve, he worked tirelessly, attempting to bring people together, listening to their stories, and trying to make peace.

Steve was unaware of the toll that these roles had been taking on his health over the years. Once again, he had become hyper-vigilant and anxious about all the possible things that could go wrong. He was extremely aware of the many ways situations in the congregation could fly apart and frequently woke in the middle of the night with tightness in his chest, unable to fall back to sleep due to the level of anxiety he was feeling. Pastor Steve even wound up in the emergency room, afraid that he was having a heart attack. But his symptoms weren't coronary problems. He was having a panic attack. In addition, his marriage was becoming strained—at least partially due to his inability to say "no." As Steve worked longer and longer hours, his wife and two young children became more and more resentful. His wife was no longer providing validation for him, and without meaning to, Steve turned more and more to his work to find that appreciation. Without conscious choice, Steve was back in the familiar roles that he learned growing up in his family of origin.

While Steve was certainly not guilty of boundary violations that could be seen as professional misconduct, he was violating boundaries every day in his attempt to make peace, bring people together, and help a congregation in decline turn around. He found it almost impossible to say "no" or to set limits. Of course the congregational leaders were at the same time urging him to do more and praising him for his tireless work. Steve was in trouble. His boundaries were not holding, his marriage was strained, and he was exhausted. The unresolved issues as the over-functioning child in the family of an alcoholic, along with his profound need for validation for being a peacemaker and problem solver, now intersected with a troubled, anxiety-driven congregation. Because the interaction effect is powerful, we can assume that without intervention, the situation will end badly.

Our premise is that this type of interaction between the issues of individual clergy and their congregation's dynamics makes setting ministry boundaries difficult. The story of Pastor Steve illustrates how complicated this interaction can be. The fault was not with Steve, and was not with his congregation, but rather with how his preexisting issues interacted with complicated system dynamics in his congregation. The result was a perfect storm. For this reason, setting healthy boundaries is not easy work. The issues that clergy bring to ministry have the potential to become activated by congregational dynamics.

CLERGY AND MULTIPLE SYSTEMS

In addition to the work of setting boundaries in complicated congregational systems, clergy are part of a number of systems simultaneously. For example, while attempting to lead a congregation, a minister is involved with his or her own immediate family issues, dealing with both marital issues and parenting issues. It is not uncommon for a minister to be attempting to lead a congregation through difficult times, while trying to set boundaries with a teenager, who is in trouble at school and not performing well academically. And while these pressures are going on, ministers may also have aging parents in another state requiring care. Now the minister is caught between the competing demands of at least five systems: the church system, the marital system, the parenting system, and the school system—not to mention aging parents in poor health. All of those systems want something and are putting pressure on the minister. Those pressures, especially in midlife, can be suffocating and can make it very difficult to set boundaries. Consequently, clergy are always engaged in feedback loops with a number of systems at the same time.

CLERGY AND NUCLEAR FAMILY

While clergy are dealing with difficult and anxious congregational systems, we are also dealing with our own marriages and families. This is a powerful feedback loop. Too many clergy spouses feel shortchanged and bitter about their spouse's failure to set boundaries and have the sense that the congregation functions as the pastor's lover—whose needs come before those of the spouse and family. Missed soccer games, too many late evening meetings, exhausting Sundays followed by depressed Mondays, emergency visits that take their spouse away from home, and too many phone calls during dinner all take their toll. How many clergy have heard their spouse say, "You have time for everyone but me. Maybe I could make an appointment with you and then you would listen to me." Clergy are often torn between the needs of their families and the demands of their congregations. They know that in the end neither system is

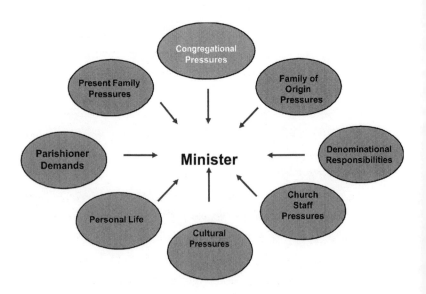

Figure 4.1.

happy. And, to complicate matters even more, pastors are some-times rewarded for being over-responsible. As a minister over-func-tions, she may be getting praise for her work in the parish and criticism at home, which, in turn, makes her over-function even more in the parish, in order to attain the internal affirmation she lacks.

The Rev. James admits that his marriage is in trouble. The con-gregation where he ministers is doing well, and he gets accolades for his sixty- and seventy-hour workweeks. He admits he does not like to go home and hear his wife criticize him for not being emo-tionally available. With some embarrassment, James reported that he provided pastoral counseling to a woman whose own marriage was in trouble and who said to him at the end of their meeting, "I hope your wife knows how lucky she is to be married to you. You are one of the kindest, most supportive men I have ever met." He then described driving home feeling good about himself, only to hear his wife say as he walked in the door, "Late again! Dinner is now cold, the kids are cranky, and I'm sick of your schedule." As we discussed in chapter 2, the congregation—or at least people in the congregation—can function as self-objects to the pastor, provid-ing the affirmation clergy lack. When parishioners function as self-objects to the pastor, professional roles and boundaries are reversed, and the pastor loses his capacity to lead the congregation. In this example, the parishioner for whom James is providing pastoral care is also functioning as a self-object for him, helping him feel a great-er sense of self-worth.

In the crucible of family and congregational interactions, over-functioning for the congregation and receiving the validation and mirroring that results may feel easier than working through a thorny marital issue that requires insight and change. For many clergy, negotiating between family and congregation becomes a complicat-ed boundary problem. They are caught between the demands of family and the demands of congregation. Instead of addressing these competing demands, many clergy turn back to the congregation to receive the support they are not receiving at home.

FAMILY OF ORIGIN

At the same time they are negotiating between the needs of their congregations and current families, clergy have to deal with the legacies of their original families. Our families present us with challenges with both vertical and horizontal dimensions. The horizontal dimension reflects current stressors, such as aging parents, health crises, and difficult siblings. The vertical dimension describes the process by which roles, triangles, and anxiety are passed on from one generation to the next. The horizontal dimension also includes the all-too-frequent role of the clergyperson as the over-responsible member of their family of origin—a role that does not end just because they are adults. Parents and siblings continue to call. For many clergy, midlife is a collision of multiple stressors. When clergy are caught between aging parents in need of care, a developing family with adolescents who might be pushing the boundaries, and a demanding congregation, we can easily become overwhelmed.

Sarah's experience was a perfect example of a horizontal challenge. She was the senior minister in a growing suburban congregation. On the surface, everything looked great. Her ministerial colleagues were envious of the seeming health of her congregation and the many programs she had launched. However, her stress levels were getting out of control. Her two children were adolescents, and her son was testing all the family boundaries. He announced defiantly that he no longer believed in God and would not attend church or youth group. Her husband had just been promoted to a managerial post and was working longer and longer hours. Her aging mother had become increasingly frail, and Sarah knew she would have to make complicated decisions about her future care. Sarah felt constant guilt about not being able to be present or provide the care that her parents, who lived in Florida, needed, and she worried about when she might be able to spend time with them. And while her congregation was doing well, they are now faced with a major task: renovating their educational wing and fellowship hall and trying to raise the money to do so.

Where in the world does she begin to set boundaries? To whom can she say "no"? She is feeling pressure from three systems simultaneously. Being a people pleaser, Sarah hates to disappoint anyone. The thought that she cannot manage all the balls in the air and that she is going to have to make painful decisions to set limits is overwhelming. If she sets boundaries in any of these three systems, someone will be unhappy with her, which will stir up one of her core issues: her need to please everyone. Pastor Sarah feels flooded with anxiety when she thinks of disappointing anyone in any of these overlapping systems.

The family of origin also has a vertical dimension. Most people are not aware of the legacy of multigenerational anxiety that we inherit. However, this multigenerational legacy is extremely important for understanding leadership styles. The vertical flow impacts how clergy lead during times of anxiety. Will they become reactive, cut off, get involved in triangles? The answer is to some extent influenced by multigenerational patterns that are passed on through vertical transmission.

Many clergy can talk about their Myers–Briggs type and may even be able to describe their leadership style. Rarely, however, are we aware that the presence or absence of anxiety leads to two distinctly different leadership styles. While a minister may pride himself or herself on having a calm, nonreactive, vision-oriented leadership style, a different style emerges when anxiety ratchets up. Under intense anxiety, a more primitive style of leadership emerges, frequently connected to our role in our family of origin.

The Rev. Stan was a model minister. He kept up with regular continuing education, was respected in his denomination, and for five years had served First Church, a very successful parish that was growing numerically and developing spiritually. However, in his sixth year with the congregation, a controversy emerged about the congregation's vision for the future and how to utilize their endowment. Anxiety began to increase. Parishioners began to withhold their pledges. As he had in the past, the Rev. Stan tried to lead creatively, focus on process, and stay nonreactive. However, stress mounted in the overlapping relationship systems Stan was part of. Congregational finances became tighter. Stan and his wife began to struggle with their seventeen-year-old son. Stan's father was diagnosed with cancer. A perfect storm was brewing. The Rev. Stan's reactive responses increased, and he began to cut off emotionally from his wife and his congregation.

As a child, when his family's anxiety became too toxic, Stan would retreat to his room, turn on his stereo, and tune the world out. He handled difficulty with his family of origin by emotionally shutting down and cutting off. He was now repeating the same strategy with negative consequences.

Stan was faced with an interaction effect—trying to cope with a congregational conflict at the same time as family crisis—which together triggered increased anxiety in Stan, his family, and his congregation. Stan's normal leadership style is no longer working, and his default style has kicked in. Not only is Stan's wife noticing the difference, but also people in the congregation are noticing. Stan is more withdrawn, looks tired, and is becoming more reactive than has been usual for him over his six years in this parish.

However, the story became more complicated. As Stan began to cut off and shut down, he became lonelier and began to look forward to discussions with a female member of his board who was extremely supportive and empathic. While nothing inappropriate had happened, Stan was on a slippery slope that could have devastating consequences.

All of us are embedded in numerous systems. Clergy must deal with congregational and family dynamics, not to mention family-of-origin, community and denominational pressures, friendships, and the need to have a personal life. Balancing all of these relationships and needs is a monumental task. Just in the congregation alone, the minister must negotiate numerous feedback loops. She is in relationship with administrative boards, congregational secretaries, choir directors and organists, the women's group and men's group, people who want pastoral care, members who require pastoral care, people who wish everything would go back to the good old days. . . . The list goes on and on.

Setting effective boundaries requires the minister to know the legacies of his family of origin—such as the unmet needs for validation and mirroring, as well as the way he was often validated for the role he played in his family of origin. But it also requires the ability to accurately read the congregational system he is part of, assess the congregation's level of anxiety, and recognize when parishioners are catching the contagion of the anxious system. At the same time, leaders of his congregation can facilitate the minister's boundary setting by learning to recognize their own levels of anxiety and helping set clear boundaries—protecting his days off, refraining from contacting him at home except in emergencies, encouraging him to use all the time allotted for his vacation and continuing education, and establishing a sabbatical policy and insisting he make use of it. Obviously, most congregational leaders do not think in these progressive ways. We believe that it is important for denominational leaders to provide board training to help educate board members about recognizing anxiety and supporting healthy boundaries for their ministers. Clergy can spell out these expectations and needs, as well as the likely resistance to them, when they enter a new system. And outside facilitators brought in early on can help congregations and boards to consider their role in protecting and nurturing their newly called pastoral leader.

THE PROBLEM OF EMOTIONAL CONTAGION

Understanding the family-of-origin issues that clergy bring to ministry as well as how those issues interact with the complicated issues of congregational systems is difficult on a good day. However, the greater the anxiety within the minister and in the congregation, the more difficult this becomes. The power of emotional contagion is a particularly useful concept in helping to understand what happens in times of heightened anxiety. Anxiety is highly contagious. When anxiety increases in a system, it tends to become infectious. Anxiety, like a bad case of the flu, can spread quickly, without people even knowing why they are anxious. In intervening in anxious congregations during times of crisis, I have facilitated listening groups to learn what congregants think the problem is. These listening groups can be used by ministers as a tool to help lower congregational anxiety and create better understanding. They are very simple to structure. People are encouraged to sign up in groups to give their perspective about various church issues. The minister's role is simply to facilitate the discussion, model healthy communication, and help people listen to each other. The listening process often results in people better understanding each other and in the end feeling less anxious.

Listening groups can amaze the leader and participants, as they overhear so many definitions of the problem and notice that most definitions arise from indirect information! An example of just such indirect information is the following: "I heard from Mrs. So and So that our minister did not visit Mr. X when he was sick, because it was our minister's day off." These stories spread through anxious systems like the old game of telephone so that in the end the contagion of anxiety has infected almost everyone and the concluding story bears little resemblance to the initial problem or complaint. Listening groups clarify issues of concern as well as help correct misinformation and rumors.

Contagion occurs during times of chronic anxiety. As was stated in chapter 3, chronic anxiety is the result of multiple stressors that occur over time. When people are caught in chronically anxious systems, they can lose awareness of their anxiety, since anxiety has now become their norm. The greater the anxiety and emotional contagion, the more primitive and reactive people become and the less capable of creative thinking.

Emotional contagion fuels the powerful interactions between the unresolved and often unconscious issues that clergy bring to ministry and the anxiety that is part of many congregations. It fuels the emotional reactivity that often erupts in these contexts, as clergy exhibit poor leadership and congregations project anxiety onto clergy and congregational scapegoats.

Our perspective is that clergy must be able to step back and understand the anxiety in their congregations and what congregations do when they are anxious. At the same time, they must become more aware of the issues they bring to ministry and how their leadership style shifts when they are anxious. Finally, they must be able to observe how their issues are intersecting with the issues of the congregation and producing a powerful interaction effect.

Without clear boundaries, this work will never take place. Ministers who have put in place time for study and prayer, time to meet with a mentor, coach, or therapist, or time to be part of a clergy group will be in a much better position to better observe themselves and their congregations and shift their leadership style accordingly. The power of emotional contagion and the types of interactions that we have described cannot be underestimated. It is all too easy even for the most creative minister to be drawn into reactive responses. Clear boundaries can make an enormous difference in the health of clergy and congregations. Finding support for setting boundaries is the subject of our final chapter.

PRACTICE

1. Create a bar graph showing the level of anxiety in each of your overlapping relational systems. If 0 is no anxiety and 10 is so anxious you are in a state of constant hyper-vigilance, how anxious is your current family? Your congregation? Your family of origin? You? Identify other systems that are significant to you, and add a bar graph for each one.

2. Identify the sources of anxiety in each of these systems. Where do you see interaction effects (that is, where does the anxiety in one system cause anxiety to ratchet up in another system)?

3. What legacies do you carry from your family of origin? For example, what roles did you play? How did you cope when the family was under stress? What needs for validation and admiration were left untended? How are these legacies helpful in your identity as minister? How might they be problematic?

4. What challenges are on the horizon for you on a vertical level (roles, triangles, and anxiety passed down to you from earlier generations) and on the horizontal level (from your role in your family of origin)?

5. What is your leadership style when you are under acute stress? Is your leadership style different when the stress becomes chronic?

6. How do you know when you are becoming reactive during times of anxiety? Where in your body do you feel it?

5

SAYING NO TO SAY YES

David Brooks, a *New York Times* columnist and frequent commentator on American politics, government, and culture, wrote a column entitled "The Leadership Revival."[1] Brooks reminds us of moments of "spine-tingling transcendence" in public life, such as Dr. Martin Luther King Jr.'s mountaintop sermon or Nelson Mandela's 1964 speech from the dock. The result of such moments, Brooks asserts, is nothing less than epic. These events have inspired many to enter leadership in the public arena. Clergy too have been inspired by similar moments, responding to a call from God to enter ministry. But as Brooks asks: "How do you execute that sort of vision? How do you translate the poetry of high aspiration into the prose of effective governance?" The same question applies to clergy trying to translate "high aspiration" into effective congregational leadership.

Like any good homiletician, Brooks offers three suggestions: apprentice to a master craftsman, take a reality bath in a foreign culture in order to gain perspective on your own, and finally, this advice: "Close off your options." As Brooks notes, "People in public life live in a beckoning world. They have an array of opportunities. They naturally want to keep all their options open. The shrewd strategists tell them to make a series of tepid commitments to see what pans out. Hedge your bets. Play it smart."

But when we hedge our bets, we spread ourselves too thin and dissipate our energy, unable to communicate our initial inspiration. Brooks's bias is toward focus and narrowing options: to say "no" to some of the innumerable requests filling our days in order to say "yes" to what we truly value. Unless you are willing to close off your options, Brooks instructs, you "never put your full force behind any cause. You make your own trivial career the object of your attention, not the vision that inspired you in the first place. *Only the masters of renunciation leave an imprint, only those who can say a hundred Nos for the sake of an overwhelming Yes* [our emphasis]."

In this chapter, we offer the most compelling reason possible for setting boundaries. Boundaries are essential for the sake of the initial vision that prompted our calls to ministry, that overwhelming Yes. We wrote this book not because we have a fascination with rules but because we have a conviction: ultimately, setting boundaries is about excellence in ministry. By narrowing our options enough that we are able to serve competently and fulsomely, we more fully embody the overwhelming Yes that inspired us to begin with.

We begin by looking at the significant goal that inspires setting boundaries: what some call "pastoral excellence." We'll explore the practical implications of the theories offered in earlier chapters for setting boundaries. We'll look at practices that can help us set and maintain appropriate limits over the long haul, such as coaching, therapy, family-of-origin groups, clergy peer learning groups, and spiritual practice. And finally, we'll consider how congregations can create an environment that respects and fosters clergy boundaries.

> ## Practice Tips
>
> - Recall the moments—perhaps of "spine-tingling transcendence"—that led you to enter the ministry. Write about the vision that still compels you, provides an "overwhelming Yes."
> - What did you originally hope you would be doing in ministry that would help implement that vision? How does that compare to what you are currently doing?
> - Identify the options you need to "close off" to deepen your commitment to this vision.

"PASTORAL EXCELLENCE" AS A NEW NARRATIVE FOR MINISTRY

Narrowing our options and setting boundaries enables us to deepen our expertise. As Malcolm Gladwell notes in *Outliers*, his book about exceptional performance, success in any field is largely a function of practicing a given task a total of around 10,000 times.[2] Gladwell quotes neurologist Daniel Levitin's book *This Is Your Brain on Music: The Science of a Human Obsession*: "In study after study . . . this number comes up again and again. No one has yet found a case in which true world-class expertise was accomplished in less time. It seems that it takes the brain this long to assimilate all that it needs to know to achieve true mastery."[3] However, we cannot become an expert at anything if we are responding to everything. And we can't make the choices the gospel requires if we are worried about staying out of conflicts or keeping the peace with the very people who pay our salaries. Something more is required of us if we are to become experts, if we are to have the kind of internal self-cohesion and integrity that enable us to make harrowing choices.

What is that something more? For the past decade, one phrase that has captured that "something more" has been "pastoral excellence." We assert that our capacity to say "no" is directly linked to our potential to develop the expertise and self-cohesion required to become excellent pastors.

What do we mean by the term "pastoral excellence?"

In 2002, the Lilly Endowment's Religion Division—under the guidance of Senior Vice President Craig Dykstra and Program Officer John Wimmer—launched a twelve-year, $84 million grant program called Sustaining Pastoral Excellence (SPE). As Dykstra noted in a presentation to a meeting with many of the sixty-three project awardees,[4] the Religion Division's goal was to strengthen local congregations. A crucial aspect of doing so was to enhance the quality of pastoral ministry—so they decided to focus on "pastoral excellence." What "pastoral excellence" means was never stipulated by the SPE program and intentionally so, according to Dykstra. "We understand that 'excellence' is better described or portrayed than defined or measured. As with 'beauty,' we know it when we see it— at least if we have 'eyes to see.'" A program that reached 10 percent of United States congregations and over forty-eight thousand pastoral leaders, "pastoral excellence" became a term describing "a new narrative of ministry." In his presentation, Dykstra elaborated some of the contours of pastoral excellence: "If Christian people are truly to hear the Good News and to live faithfully in response, they need pastors who know the Christian gospel in their own heart of hearts, who are well-equipped to teach it and preach it, and who are effectively able to help shape the corporate life and ministry of the congregation into a vital community of faith. Some congregations can survive weak pastoral leadership for a while—but not for long. And we know that really fine pastors are indispensable to the long-term thriving not only of any particular congregation, but also of the large, broad, interconnected community of faith as a whole."[5]

Consultants who helped shape the SPE program were somewhat wary of the term "pastoral excellence." The word "excellence" is potentially subject to cultural notions that may not conform to theological interpretations of excellence. In a book commissioned by the Lilly Endowment, Greg Jones, then dean and professor of theology at Duke Divinity School, and Kevin Armstrong, senior pastor of North United Methodist Church in Indianapolis, responded to this concern. An uncritical church has adopted cultural notions of excellence, they argue—such as competition, achievement, winners and losers, success—"the essence of personal coaching."[6] In contrast, the authors reclaim a theological meaning of excellence, such as that found in Philippians 2:6–11 or in Simone Weil's understanding of the cross as the intersection between creation and Creator, human life and God's life, tragedy and hope, strength and weakness, death and life. As they write: "Resurrecting excellence does not depend on moral perfection, workaholic behavior, or individual effectiveness. It depends on the intersection of human creativity with divine creativity and on communities of people who join together in a journey of faithfulness to God's inbreaking kingdom."[7] Resurrecting excellence clarifies both the distortions and the gifts of three understandings of ordination: calling, profession, and office. At its best, a calling is attentiveness, listening and learning. At its worst, a calling is therapy or self-denial. The gift of a profession is practical wisdom; its distortion is careerism. The office of pastoral leadership at its best is administration and growth in following Jesus; distorted, it leads to authoritarianism, hierarchy, and bureaucracy.

In a comprehensive study of pastoral leaders and congregations, also commissioned by Lilly, Jack Carroll, director of the Pulpit and Pew Project at Duke Divinity School, takes a practical look at the underpinnings of pastoral excellence—the demographics, work habits, leadership style, commitment, satisfaction, and health of pastors.[8] He concludes with recommended practices for clergy to take responsibility for growth in pastoral excellence:

- Develop and practice spiritual disciplines
- Reflect on your practice of ministry
- Become lifelong learners
- Nurture friendships
- Maintain appropriate boundaries between personal/family life and work
- Engage in diligent physical and emotional self-care
- Do not contribute to a culture of complaint or denial

Practice Tips

- What is your definition of pastoral excellence?
- Reflect on Jack Carroll's suggested list of ways to nurture pastoral excellence. Where do you long for more depth? What do you need to change—internally, externally—to have room for the "yes" you are longing to practice?

If these are the practices that contribute to pastoral excellence, they also provide clues to the boundaries needed in our ministries, in our lives. In which of these practices do we need to go deeper? What's getting in our way? Are our needs for validation or to be needed proving to be obstacles to deepening our commitment to these practices?

One feature of the SPE Program was highlighted as an experiment in strengthening pastors of excellence: peer learning groups. Over sixteen thousand pastoral leaders participated in some form of peer learning groups during the SPE Program. As the SPE website notes, "these groups provide opportunities for intellectual, vocational, spiritual, physical and emotional support, education and encouragement. Pastoral leaders study the Bible and theology, practice spiritual disciplines, build pastoral skills and participate in retreats, much-deserved relaxation and/or renewing travel. In these projects, they are encouraged and enabled to design and implement programs that will help them sustain pastoral excellence over the long haul."[9]

How do peer groups help us solidify pastoral excellence? How do they help us create and maintain the kind of boundaries needed for deepening our practices? Are there groups that are more helpful and groups that are less helpful? Austin Presbyterian Seminary's College of Pastoral Leaders was funded by Lilly to explore these questions. Janet Maykus, principal of the College of Pastoral Leaders, and Penny Marler, professor of religion at Samford University, conducted the evaluation. Maykus and Marler utilized two national surveys of religious professionals, as well as a survey of several thousand pastors who participated in the SPE peer learning groups.

Among their findings are some indicators that describe pastoral excellence. For example, congregations whose pastors participated in peer groups are more likely to cultivate congregations that the researchers describe as "a culture of involvement," including the following characteristics:

- Actively assimilate newcomers
- Rotate lay people in leadership roles more frequently
- Support youth ministry
- Participate in community service [10]

In addition, the researchers concluded that the longer a pastor participates in a peer group that is led by a trained facilitator and/or has a structured curriculum, the more likely that the pastor's congregation will be experiencing numerical growth.

From our perspective, the most important finding in the research was that clergy peer groups enabled clergy to set and maintain the limits they knew were essential for pastoral excellence. Participants in peer learning groups were better at balancing personal and ministry responsibilities than colleagues who did not participate. Maykus and Marler note that "reports from focus group interviews with our five representative SPE peer groups indicate that belonging to a peer group *legitimizes* activities that many of pastoral leaders intuitively knew were necessary for a long and vital ministry but found difficult to squeeze into their schedules. Time of Sabbath, fellowship with friends, creative endeavors, prayer, and laughter became parts of their pastoral rhythms and therefore parts of the rhythms of their calls. . . . When pastoral leaders internalize this rhythm and repeat the pattern, . . . the benefits, our analysis shows, can be quite tangible."[11] In comparing pastors who were in peer groups to those who were not, pastors who regularly took a day off were more than two times more likely to be participants in peer groups and to say that maintaining a private life separate from work life was not a problem.

Peer groups benefit clergy in many important ways. According to Maykus and Marler: "We can say with a high degree of confidence that if a peer group has certain characteristics [a trained facilitator and a structured curriculum or intentional learning plan], it will: (a) result in a feeling of renewal in a pastoral leader's ministry; (b) have a positive impact on his or her family and close friends; (c) lead to enhanced creativity; and/or (d) produce greater intimacy with God."[12] The researchers also identified specific factors that led to a superior peer-group experience, which we will discuss later on in this chapter.

Participation in a peer group brings with it the need to resolve conflict. For over the life of the group, conflict will surface—just as in any group. Being able to resolve the conflict positively, participants stated, inspired them to be "bolder and more secure leaders. They also reported that participation in SPE peer groups helped them deal with conflict in their congregations."[13] We cannot emphasize enough the benefits of these support groups and believe they are an essential part of setting boundaries in the interest of pastoral excellence. Sometimes local pastoral counseling centers sponsor clergy peer groups or may have staff willing and able to do so. Sometimes a group of pastors hire a facilitator from among psychotherapists or mentors they know. Denominations sometimes sponsor peer groups, although many clergy find it helpful to be in a group where multiple denominational perspectives are represented. Appendix 2 offers suggestions on how to start such a group if it is difficult to find one.

In summary, Maykus and Marler comment: "It is a healthy balance of relational, spiritual, and instrumental interests and peer group practices, in the end, that yields renewed energy for and commitment to ministry for any pastoral leader."[14]

Practice Tips

- What kinds of support structures could help you engage more deeply in the ways you practice pastoral excellence?

HOW TO SAY "NO" TO SAY "YES": BOUNDARIES IN ACTION

We began this chapter with David Brooks's references to Dr. Martin Luther King Jr. and Nelson Mandela as examples of highly inspirational leaders who created both moments of transcendence as well as movements that accomplished great things. Certainly both reflect

a rare type of excellent spiritual leadership that impacted generations and helped create significant transformation in their countries
and in the world. While most have heard their amazing speeches,
and felt electrified while listening, it is important to remember that
both needed to say "no" to a number of things in their lives in order
to say "yes" to a compelling vision of change. Dr. King often predicted an early death for himself as the cost of living out his vision.
Nelson Mandela, despite profound injustice and a lengthy prison
term, was able to say "no" to bitterness and rage, in order to say
"yes" to his vision for South Africa. Much could be said about both
leaders' ability to say "no" for the sake of saying "yes" to their
visions. Dietrich Bonhoeffer talks about this in his well-known book
The Cost of Discipleship.

Excellence in ministry is that ability to say "no" even when it is
difficult. And it is the ability to also be very clear about what we are
saying "yes" to. This requires high levels of differentiation of self.

SELF-DIFFERENTIATION

Perhaps one of the ways peer groups help clergy is to hold them
accountable in implementing familiar advice. Most of us have attended workshops on self-care and burnout prevention and hear the
same recommendations over and over. "Take a sabbatical, get exercise, spend time with family, cultivate friends apart from the congregation, read more, eat a balanced diet, practice spiritual disciplines, go on retreat."

The problem with all of this well-meaning advice is that most
clergy already know what they should be doing but find it quite
difficult to find the time and energy to do the very things that will
make them healthier and might enhance their ministry. Peer groups
provide a support network to explore both healthy strategies that

will lead to excellence and support for setting the boundaries that will help them get there.

Peer groups also help us work on one especially crucial aspect of setting boundaries—understanding and strengthening our level of differentiation, a concept originally developed by Murray Bowen. For clergy to be successful and develop excellence in ministry, they must also move toward improved levels of differentiation. Clergy groups help us be accountable and support and challenge us. Clergy groups may also provide both support and help for differentiation work especially when led by a trained facilitator. Many clergy have also benefited from working with the insights of two students of Murray Bowen, Rabbi Edwin H. Friedman and the Rev. Peter Steinke,[15] and may have even used these books within clergy groups.

THE ROLE OF DIFFERENTIATION IN SETTING BOUNDARIES

Differentiation is defined as "the ability to be in emotional contact with others yet still autonomous in one's emotional functioning."[16] It is the ability to maintain emotional objectivity in the midst of a system in emotional turmoil but still actively connect to people in the system. From a boundary-awareness perspective, a differentiated minister will have both the strength to set firm and clear limits, while staying emotionally connected to key members of the congregation, even in times of great anxiety. Some clergy find it easy to say "no" but have difficulty maintaining emotional connection to congregants while doing so. Others stay emotionally connected but have great difficulty saying "no" to things that move them away from creativity. Doing both simultaneously is complicated.

Setting limits begins with the necessity of being clear about one's vision of excellence in ministry. Without clarity about what we are saying "yes" to, there is little point in saying "no." This is especially complicated in small parishes where clergy are expected to be generalists and be good at everything from preaching to pastoral care, to administration, to proofreading the bulletin, and making sure the heating system works in the winter.

Bowen's concept of differentiation provides a map for practice of setting boundaries. Murray Bowen[17] originally described a scale of differentiation ranging from one to one hundred with higher scores representing higher levels of differentiation. People who have a poorly differentiated self are dependent on the acceptance and approval of others and tend to adjust their actions on the basis of others' approval or expectation. In the same way, an extreme rebel within a family is not differentiated but simply takes an oppositional position in regard to others. Neither the rebel nor the person desperate for approval is differentiated. On the other hand, people who are more differentiated can stay calm in the midst of anxiety and criticism, can separate feelings from thinking so their decisions are not clouded by emotionality, and can make calm decisions guided by their thoughtfully developed core values. They can do this while remaining in emotional connection to people. Obviously, becoming differentiated in this way is the work of a lifetime. If differentiation can be described as calming your own emotional reactivity while people around you are becoming reactive, while at the same time staying in emotional contact with those people, it becomes clear how difficult a process it is. While Bowen has at times been accused of being too cognitive, and downplaying emotion, that critique misunderstands what he was saying. He was actually describing how important it is to observe and think about one's feelings before expressing those feelings reactively, especially for those in positions of leadership. Most of us would admit that some of the biggest leadership mistakes we have made have occurred when we were depleted and became emotionally reactive.

Undifferentiated leaders allow the congregation or group to set their agenda and then try to become what others expect them to be. Obviously, excellence will never result. Differentiated leaders set boundaries around time and congregational expectations in order to carefully discern their leadership style, what their gifts are, and what excellence would mean to them. They are able to carefully convey this vision to board members and then collaboratively set boundaries to allow them to live into that vision, understanding that it will involve saying "no" to things that get in the way.

Practice Tips

- Take time with a coach, or during a sabbatical, or in the midst of your spiritual practice, and write a brief summary of your vision for yourself in terms of pastoral excellence.
- Next, identify what is blocking your implementation of that vision.
- What action steps will need to be taken to set boundaries in order to live out that vision?

One of the significant blocks to clear vision in ministry and maintaining the necessary boundaries to implement that vision is what Bowen referred to as multigenerational transmission. (The Old Testament referred to this as the sins of the fathers being passed on for generations.) Multigenerational transmission, as discussed in chapter 3, is the process by which roles, relationship patterns, and anxiety can be passed on for generations. For clergy, the concept of how family roles are passed on generationally is especially important since family roles have a major impact on leadership styles. The child who was the over-responsible member of the family, and was praised for doing everything, will have great difficulty in pastoral leadership saying "no." The family peacemaker will spend too much time as a leader attempting to bring people together but may neglect any compelling vision other then helping people get along. The lost child, the child who received little or no attention or validation, may use ministry as a way to seek validation and therefore have great difficulty setting boundaries. These family roles can shape leadership in such a way that it is both difficult to set clear boundaries and even more difficult to pursue excellence. And as we have discussed repeatedly, during times of anxiety, these old family roles become even more pronounced. Unless these family roles are understood and reworked, leadership may be ineffective, and setting boundaries will prove difficult.

Practice Tips

- Think about the role you played in your family of origin.
- How does that role impact your current leadership style?
- How does anxiety impact that style?
- Work with a coach or therapist on finding ways of better understanding and changing the impact of your family role on your leadership style.

Most attempts to create change and to set limits in order to pursue excellence will meet with some resistance, which must be managed. It is not enough to simply say "no" without managing the feelings of people and groups who are not supportive of the changes being made. The literature on emotional intelligence (EI)[18] adds more detail to what Bowen was describing with the concept of differentiation and is an important part of this process. It explains how tiring ministry can be since it constantly involves both recognizing and regulating what you are feeling, recognizing what others are feeling, and then regulating the interaction between you and others. EI expert Daniel Goleman states that emotional intelligence has several dimensions. Simply stated, emotional intelligence is the ability to be both self-aware as well as socially aware. Both involve several components. Being self-aware means being both aware of what one is feeling at any given time, as well as being able to regulate those feelings. Kerr and Bowen refer to one aspect of this as having an internal anxiety meter so one is always aware of the level of one's anxiety in interpersonal settings so as to not inadvertently become reactive. If the anxiety meter is in the "red zone," it is essential not to act reactively but to find a way to slow things down. Emotionally intelligent leaders try to be in touch with what they are feeling and regulate those feelings so as to stay both clear and connected to the people around them.

Imagine a highly conflicted board meeting. Pastor Alan is not well differentiated and not always self-aware. He becomes increasingly agitated and defensive as board members review his preaching. Finally, he blurts out, "No one is going to tell me what to preach or how to preach. I will preach what God tells me to preach." The tension in the room and in the board meeting becomes even hotter. Board members are looking at each other uncomfortably, not knowing how to respond and becoming even more agitated. Pastor Alan was unaware of how irritated he had become and so was unable to regulate what he was feeling and then spoke from that irritation. As a result, he became even more alienated from his board. From a boundary-awareness perspective, Pastor Alan means well. He is trying to set boundaries to allow him to pursue his passion for excellence in preaching. However, his reactivity is blocking board members from even understanding what he is trying to do. Emotional intelligence for clergy leaders means both knowing what you feel in any given situation and then being able to regulate what you are feeling in the midst of managing networks of relationships.

Consider Pastor Beth's response to the same stressors. She recognized her own growing defensiveness and agitation with what her board was saying and decided this was not a good time to speak. She listened to the concerns of the board and then tried to summarize what their concerns were, asking if she was accurately hearing what they were saying. Reflective listening allowed her to relax a bit and to avoid blurting out a response in the midst of her agitation. She then assured the board she would give some thought to their concerns and would talk more to them about it at the next meeting but made sure that everyone in the room felt that she heard their concerns. Pastor Beth then suggested having breakfast the following week with the board chair to fully process what she was hearing from the board. This nonreactive strategy reduced the anxiety in the room, kept her well connected to the group, while not simply caving in to what the board wanted. Essentially, she was doing four things simultaneously: recognizing her own emotions, regulating those emotions, connecting to the thoughts and feelings of her board members, and using social skills to manage these relationships.

Practice Tips

- Try to identify a time when you became highly defensive when your leadership or pastoral skills were being challenged. How did your anxiety manifest? Did you become defensive or agitated or just shut down? What would you have done differently if you could have recognized the level of your anxiety?

Differentiation in times of low anxiety is not difficult. However, in times of heightened anxiety, it is much more difficult. Goleman refers to this as "low road circuitry," which acts at high speed often under conscious awareness. It implies that too much happens automatically and without much critical thinking. As we described in chapter 3, the chronic anxiety of many congregations runs on low-road circuitry—like an underground railroad. And it is contagious. To shift to the high road, which provides us with more conscious choices, clergy must be able to be in touch with what is happening on the low road, what they are feeling, and then find differentiated strategies for keeping things on the high road. The high road means we are able to respond creatively, not reactively, even in the midst of emotional contagion. This is an important clergy boundary that is rarely discussed. Essentially it is a self-boundary aimed at keeping leaders from being impacted by low-road circuitry and staying differentiated to keep things on the high road. The goal is not simply to have good boundaries, and say "no" to overwork, but to be differentiated enough and self-aware enough to say "yes" to growth for yourself and the congregation. Healthy boundaries will keep us connected to our overwhelming "Yes."

Differentiation is also the ability to shift the discussion and process to the high road in the midst of heightened anxiety. It is not enough to simply be empathic: empathy can actually limit leadership.[19] Goleman suggests that leaders need not only empathy but also "social facility."[20] He summarizes this thought by saying, "simply sensing how another feels, or knowing what they think or intend, does not guarantee fruitful interactions. Social facility builds on social awareness to allow smooth, effective interactions."[21] This includes the ability to interact smoothly at the nonverbal level, shape the outcome of social interactions, as well as care about people's needs and act accordingly. This "social facility" is what helps shape congregations and is an essential part of effective leadership. It is built on the capacity to stay on the high road even in the midst of chronic anxiety.

Boundary setting based on improved differentiation is difficult to
learn. Seminary trains the neocortex with courses in homiletics,
pastoral care, church history, exegesis, and so forth. However, differentiation and emotional intelligence are related to the limbic system, the seat of the emotions, which is neglected in seminary
coursework. Describing the concept of differentiation is easier than
living as a differentiated self. The best way to understand the complexity of the concept and to experience being on the "low road" is
to imagine going home to your entire family for the holidays. What
a training for the limbic system! How many days can you remain
nonreactive without getting hooked by siblings, parents, or other
relatives and beginning to feel like you are fifteen again? Old
"dances" die hard, and family members know how to bring out the
worst in each other. But differentiation is not simply about remaining nonreactive or avoiding getting pulled into old dances or roles.
It is also the capacity to maintain one-to-one relationships with key
members of the family without getting caught in those old reactive
dances. In Bowen-based therapy or effective clergy groups, clergy
do not simply explore their family legacies. Rather, they are
coached to go home, move toward anxious relationships, and practice not only becoming emotionally nonreactive but also engaging
more intimately in important relationships. In the language of emotional intelligence, this is not cognitive training but training the
limbic system through exposure to anxious interpersonal situations.

Practice Tips

- Think about the last time you returned to your family of origin.
- What "buttons" got pushed and by whom?
- Once you were "hooked," what happened? Pretend you can watch it as a video. What do you notice about your style once you became reactive?

Pastor Don, for example, believed that by going home to his fundamentalist family and describing the progressive theology he was reading and taking a proud position on controversial social issues, he was being differentiated. In reality, he was demonstrating a type of emotional reactivity. He was not trying to understand his family members and was not working on deeper understandings and connections with family members. Pastor Don's reactive position (which he naively thought was differentiation) created a type of emotional cutoff preventing him from getting close to any family members, while feeling proud that he was demonstrating how different he was from his family. Not surprisingly, this same style was creating problems with key board members in his congregation. Pastor Don was proud of his ability to say "no" to certain committees he did not want to be part of but did so more reactively, thereby alienating key church members. Saying "no" in a reactive way often misses what the group (often boards or committees) are concerned or frightened about. Saying "no" reactively is often an angry "no" to a request, as opposed to responding in a way that stays connected. For example, "I can appreciate that you want me to spend more time visiting parishioners and certainly don't want to minimize how important that is, but at the same time, I need time to focus on the priorities we established for the year." Fortunately, the clergy group Don was part of was able to gently challenge what he was doing and could see how his reactive style was creating alienation. They urged him to find a therapist/coach who was familiar with Bowen principles. He was helped by both his therapist and his group to begin building a very different type of relationship with his family by working at nonreactively getting to know family members, without giving up who he was. His clergy group helped him apply those principles to his congregation, and he began to see that, in order to lead effectively, he needed to make a significant shift in leadership style. His therapist helped him to understand that he was replicating his reactive style that he had used to deal with his family and helped him build some tools to handle conflict differently. These involved learning to stay in touch with what he was feeling, slow down when he felt anxious or angry, and role-play responses that kept him better connected to key people.

Unfortunately, it is often difficult for clergy to know how to find a therapist who is acquainted with the overlapping systems of congregations, families, and selves. We believe that it is helpful for each area judicatory to have a solid referral list of good therapists for clergy to consult with that are trained in this type of work. You can also narrow your search by asking psychotherapists if they have experience in family, systems, or Bowenian types of therapy.

A significant part of training in Bowen family systems is not just understanding theory but also being part of a family-of-origin group, where participants are coached to go home frequently and understand themselves in the context of a multigenerational family. The work is experiential, not simply cognitive; going home helps us work on differentiation by building nonreactive relationships with family members, stepping out of old triangles and old roles. It takes us beyond the old joke about psychoanalysis: "After ten years of therapy, I can talk about my father—I still can't talk to him, but I can talk about him." Bowen-based therapy aims at doing the work "live." Shifting dynamics *in situ* improves differentiation because reactivity is managed in the moment it is occurring and with the very person triggering the anxiety. In fact, many Bowen-based therapists believe that traditional therapy creates a situation where individuals talk to their therapists about their "dysfunctional families," thereby creating yet another triangle where the family will look even more negative. It is all too easy to talk about difficult family members or even complicated parishioners to a well-meaning empathic therapist. However, the therapist is only hearing one side, and if they inadvertently appear to agree about how difficult the family member or parishioner is, a triangle is created. This lowers anxiety initially, but in the end, the primary relationship does not get worked on. In the case of clergy, when a triangle is created, an opportunity to grow in leadership and the ability to set clear boundaries is lost. A Bowen-based therapist will always coach the person they are working with to move toward the anxiety and toward the relationship as a necessary step to growing more differentiated.

Working on differentiation for clergy leaders means also recognizing the blocks to differentiation in the interest of making creative changes. Pastor Sarah was a prime example. Growing up in a large family, she was the "good girl" who did everything right and was viewed by her family as the most responsible member. She received constant validation from her parents for the good choices she made and for being so much more responsible than her siblings.

Not surprisingly, this pattern followed her in ministry. Pastor Sarah tried hard to please everyone and worked tirelessly to keep all the members of her rural congregation happy. It was very difficult for her to say "no" to anything. In fact, just thinking about setting limits and saying "no" created significant anxiety. Yet the harder she worked, the more unsatisfied she became. After three years of ministry, she began to feel like she was in the wrong profession and was not putting much time into doing any of the things she looked forward to while in seminary.

Fortunately, she received some excellent advice from some trusted colleagues in her clergy group and sought out a therapist who was well acquainted with some of the unique issues clergy struggle with. Pastor Sarah learned to take more "differentiated positions" and was encouraged to say "no" to things that distracted her from her passions. Initially, the therapeutic work was exhausting. Pastor Sarah acknowledged that she was often unable to state what she was really passionate about because the thought of making changes caused significant anxiety in people in her congregation. She struggled with the thought that making changes would leave some members disappointed with her and that people would be let down. Gradually, Pastor Sarah began to realize how much she needed affirmation and to be liked. She found therapy to be difficult work and learned that change was slow. She needed the patient coaching of her therapist to support her both in defining her ministry strengths, as well as coping with the anxiety that followed whenever she felt she was disappointing people.

As Pastor Sarah began to realize just how much she needed affirmation and began to share some of her insights with trusted colleagues in her clergy group, she experienced their support to help her continue to "hold on to herself" and become firmer about what she was really passionate about in her ministry. She was able to use her strong emotional intelligence to both set limits and actively engage people in a way that enlisted their support. She began wisely by talking to her board about how together they needed to reset priorities for her ministry. She shared with them some of her passion for some new and creative programs. She asked for their help in deciding what activities she could step back from in order to focus on priorities. Initially her board was supportive and helpful, and slowly, she began to regain her passion for ministry. Pastor Sarah's preaching and worship began to improve, and she was able to initiate some new, creative ministry programs.

However, that was not the end of the story. At the same time, she continued to wrestle with her need to please people. In particular, she struggled with the chair of her administrative board, who was quite demanding. Saying "no" to her was especially difficult. Pastor Sarah and her therapist spent time role-playing how best to respond, and then processing the difficult feelings that emerged. Sarah was engaged in insight-oriented therapy: as she gained insight, she also practiced setting limits and boundaries with the coaching of her therapist. The support of both her therapist and clergy group proved invaluable. Sarah's need to be liked, her excessive needs for validation, as well as her old family role had been activated in the new congregational family. But the work she did enabled her to know herself much better and to make significant changes. Not surprisingly, as Pastor Sarah moves toward her unique pastoral excellence, her congregation is doing well.

WHAT ABOUT GENDER DIFFERENCES?

Earlier in the text, we reviewed statistics of CSM that overwhelmingly identify male clergy as the perpetrators of CSM and identify women as the victims/survivors. We wondered whether there is any connection between these statistics and the ways in which men and women may experience different disturbances in healthy selfhood. For example, if men are more likely to develop "grandiose" narcissism, sins such as pride and domination may cause them to act out sexually and in other ways. In contrast, women may develop "vulnerable" narcissism, subject to poor self-esteem diminishing rather than asserting their leadership. While these are obviously generalizations and based on conjecture rather than research, they are worthy of our reflection.

Practice Tips

- For women: is it more difficult to set boundaries because of early socialization into patterns of feminine behavior? How might you practice asserting yourself as a leader? Get more help at home? How might you identify and work with internalized criticism so that you are better able to protect your needs and lead from a healthy self?
- For men: in what ways have you learned to act rather than reflect? How might you engage in practices that help identify and protect your emotional needs? Your relationships?

SUPPORT FOR SETTING AND MAINTAINING BOUNDARIES

While sabbaticals, reading, hobbies, friends, and more are continually suggested to clergy to support their self-care and boundary work, these may not help us get to the root of our problems with saying "no." We believe that for clergy to make significant progress in setting boundaries, they need to continue to work toward increased self-differentiation and recognize personal obstacles to differentiation. Differentiation helps us observe system patterns and observe ourselves and what we are really passionate about and whether we are moving toward a "yes" of pastoral excellence. But growth in differentiation is a slow process and requires practice over time and with accountability partners. We suggest three ways to help us deepen our capacity for differentiated leadership—ways that have been tested over time and found life-changing for many clergy: facilitated/structured clergy groups, coaching/therapy, and spiritual practice.

Clergy Groups

As mentioned above, Janet Maykus and Penny Marler researched the kinds of peer learning groups that were most effective for clergy. In their study of SPE peer groups as well as clergy who responded to two national surveys, they found that peer-group involvement was high. In the two national surveys, over 75 percent of clergy respondents participated in peer groups. What did the clergy in this large pool rate as most helpful?

As you look for a clergy group, keep in mind their findings. The peer groups rated as most beneficial were structured in ways that brought about the following critical factors:

- Regular attendance
- Group meetings guided by a formal covenant
- A high-quality leader or facilitator
- Denominationally diverse
- Group intimacy and accountability
- Practices that encouraged expressing spirituality in creative ways[22]

Family-of-Origin Groups

Using a trained facilitator, clergy are helped to make a multigenerational genogram to track patterns, roles, and the flow of anxiety but then begin to make more and more trips home to work on significant relationships. The goal is never to change another but to change your pattern of relating, becoming more nonreactive and attempting to build a more intimate relationship even with difficult family members without drifting back into old roles. These types of groups have great power to help shift leadership patterns and strengthen healthy boundaries.

Coaching/Therapy

It is one thing to understand the concept of differentiation but another to implement it. To learn differentiation is to move constantly toward relational anxiety. To do that without a good coach or therapist is very difficult. Our patterns are wired, and we drift onto the "low road" much too easily. The role of a therapist or coach is to help us look carefully at our gifts, at what we are passionate about, and at how our lack of boundaries might be blocking us from excellence. Not all types of therapy will help move toward excellence. Therapy that only focuses on insight may be very helpful but needs as well to hold us accountable toward making the changes that are necessary for excellence in ministry.

Therapy or coaching must focus on helping clergy understand their family backgrounds, their roles in their families, as well as understanding how they respond in times of increased anxiety or conflict. Therapy and coaching will then help clergy learn to move toward difficult people and groups using emotional intelligence, while holding onto themselves in leadership. It is not simply about being a "people pleaser." That is not leadership, as Friedman points out in his book called *A Failure of Nerve*.[23] A good coach or therapist will not only help clergy understand the issues that they bring but also will help them clarify their leadership styles, keep them in touch with their passions, and help them set limits so those passions can be pursued.

Spiritual Practices

How does nurturing spiritual practice help us create stronger boundaries? In her book *Leaders Who Last: Sustaining Yourself and Your Ministry*, the Rev. Margaret J. Marcuson,[24] teacher, coach and consultant, offers many practical suggestions for deepening our self-awareness, increasing our capacity for differentiated leadership, and assessing our congregational systems. In her final chapter, "Saying Our Prayers," Marcuson notes that "we will be better prepared to face the challenges of ministry when we adopt and develop spiritual practices that are right for us." She writes about the benefits of meditation, practicing awareness, keeping silence, praying for others, and knowing our own faith story. Whatever practice you choose, make sure you choose a practice that helps you remember and reconnect with the overwhelming Yes that inspired you to choose ministry, a practice that helps ground you in your truest self.

One practice that is worth emphasizing is meditation. Since Marcuson's book was published, and even earlier, brain researchers have been exploring the significant changes that occur with meditative practices. Among the most important for differentiation and setting boundaries: meditation enables us to become more attuned to ourselves, increasing our capacity for self-regulation. Meditation also can help us reconnect with God, with our call, and with the hopes and aspirations we have carried for ourselves and for the congregations we lead. Whether through centering prayer practices such as those taught by Thomas Keating or Basil Pennington[25] or through mystical or contemplative traditions, meditation is a spiritual practice that can help us set boundaries around our time and develop the capacities to set better boundaries in our congregations.

HOW TO SAY "NO" TO SAY "YES"—FOR PERSONNEL COMMITTEES

Personnel committees (which have different names, depending on your denominational context) can be a wonderful resource to clergy in helping them set and maintain boundaries. First, the committee must understand how important boundaries are for the sake of congregational vitality and work carefully with their minister to help set and support those boundaries. If such a committee does not exist in your congregation, ask for a model from your denominational office or from trusted clergy colleagues. If this type of committee does not exist in your congregation, make it a priority to start one. Second, very practical strategies can be implemented such as regular meetings so that some members of the congregation begin to understand the need for clergy to take care of themselves and also help monitor that self-care is taking place. Committees can provide a coach for their minister, they can encourage sabbaticals and continuing education, and they can make sure there is money for both. They can help interpret to the larger congregation why such boundaries are essential.

Successful boundaries are a team effort. It is impossible for clergy to maintain these types of boundaries alone. Working with a supportive and creative personnel committee can be enormously helpful.

BOUNDARIES AND CONGREGATIONAL VITALITY

Throughout this book, we've noted the difference for clergy and for congregations when boundaries are encouraged by both parts of the system. Many clergy have the experience of going to a workshop or continuing-education event that encourages self-care only to return to their congregation and meet resistance when they attempt to take a day away. But some congregations are learning to support boundary setting for both their clergy and lay leaders, so that lay and clergy alike are not burned out through over-functioning.

Theologian Serene Jones[26] tells the story of being part of a planning committee in her local United Church of Christ congregation. It was a lengthy process: three months of listening to the ideas of the members, three months imagining how to respond to current challenges and dreams. However, as the planning committee moved into developing strategies for all their ambitious ideas, "people's faces looked increasingly strained, attendance began to drop, and ideas flowed less freely. At the end of a painfully unproductive meeting, the convener asked a senior member of the committee what she thought about the emerging plans."

Haven't we all had this experience—watching grand ideas falter when it's time for action? Thank goodness the senior member of this committee felt the freedom to tell the truth: "'I'm sorry,' she began, 'I don't mean to be negative, but when I look at this list I feel . . . so tired.'"[27]

Honest dismay prompted the committee to step back, enter into a time of profound theological reflection, and change their focus. As Jones summarizes: "When we began to truly grasp the depth of God's love for the world and the freedom that is given to us in that love, we not only felt the burden of our list lifted from our shoulders, we simultaneously came to see our list as a joyous response to the love that so freed us." Or as another member of the committee commented: "'When we begin to see that what we do as a church doesn't matter ultimately, we are freed to see how very much our practices do matter.'"[28] An experience of feeling overwhelmed led to a time of theological reflection and discernment—where to let go and say "no," where to open up and say "yes."

Setting boundaries for clergy is a matter of becoming clear about our false understandings of ourselves, others, and God. Clergy often act as if it is our job to save the church, a lesson many of us at early ages trained for in our families of origin. Or we act as if our parishioners can save us through their admiration and validation of us, instead of relying on God's grace to save our congregations—and us.

Congregations can get caught in the same kinds of false understandings as clergy. Part of our job as clergy is to model an understanding of who saves us—and for what. It is our job to preach, teach, and live a gospel that doesn't depend on human over-functioning but on God's grace. Ultimately, such a life enables us all to become masters of renunciation: saying "a hundred nos for the sake of an overwhelming Yes."

We conclude with an example. First Presbyterian Church had just called a new minister. They were clear in their call about the gifts they were looking for. They wanted a minister who could be a visionary and help lead them to a new way of being a church that would honor their proud history. They wanted someone who had strong preaching and leadership gifts. At the same time, they were enlightened enough to know they had to protect their new minister from excessive congregational demands that would force him to be a generalist and diminish excellence. They set up a personnel committee aimed at meeting regularly with their new minister to help him define and articulate his gifts and vision and encouraged regular study leave, time for study, and urged him to be part of a clergy group. They wanted to ensure that their new minister pursued excellence rather then trying to meet everyone's demands.

One of the more creative members of the committee suggested they pay for coaching for the first two years of ministry to help the new minister better refine his gifts and pursue excellence. Finally, they found ways to regularly interpret his priorities to the congregation so that congregants would form more realistic expectations of their new minister. This involved reviewing periodically priorities for both the congregation and pastor and regular discussion of these priorities in board meetings so success could be measured. It also meant communicating these priorities to the congregation so communication stays open. While this is an example of an unusually enlightened committee, and some might say, "How can they afford this kind of focus?" the committee members would respond, "How can we afford not to provide this level of support, if we want to reinvent our church to meet the needs of the new generation?"

Ultimately, setting boundaries is about saying "no" to the things that drain our focus and saying "yes" to a call to pastoral excellence. In writing this book, our hope is that you and your congregation will find your way to practicing boundaries that enable passionate ministry in the name of an overwhelming Yes.

Appendixes

Appendix I

BOUNDARY-AWARENESS TRAINING
A Workshop Outline

This program is offered in either four-hour or eight-hour work-shops. The eight-hour time frame allows for more discussion and interaction.

PART I: WHY ARE WE HERE?

This section is an overview of the long-term problem of clergy sexual misconduct that created a need for boundary-awareness training. In this section, we examine the contributions of Marie Fortune around issues of sexual misconduct, as well as expanding the concept of Boundary Awareness to a number of other issues. Clergy are helped to see that boundaries also apply to self-care, continuing education, social media, time management, and the difficulty many clergy have saying "no" in order to say "yes" to the pursuit of excellence. It is important in this opening section for clergy to recognize a broader definition of boundaries to ensure better participation in the workshop.

Part 1 also examines statistics that compare clergy sexual misconduct to the other helping professions and then explores how the context of parish ministry creates unique boundary concerns.

Finally, ministry boundaries are defined and discussed by the group. An opening question to the group is "how many boundaries have you violated in the last week?" Gradually, participants begin to identify how they said "yes" to things they did not want to be part of, did not take days off, neglected physical exercise as well as spiritual disciplines, and so forth. This discussion begins to build buy-in for the rest of the day's agenda.

PART 2: OVERVIEW OF BOUNDARY PROBLEMS

The next session focuses on group brainstorming on types of boundary problems that clergy typically encounter, ranging from conflict-of-interest issues, to financial issues, sexual issues, the problem of congregants wanting to be friends, and the problem of regulating distance, as well as how best to handle the issue of social media and email.

Sexual-Boundary Issues

This section explores the paradigm shift that was introduced by Marie Fortune when she defined sexual contact between clergy and a parishioner not as an affair but as sexual and professional misconduct, with dynamics similar to incest. In this section, we explore differences in power and conclude that there can never be meaningful consent between clergy and congregants due to this imbalance of power.

We also explore how misconduct occurs as an outgrowth of pastoral counseling sessions.

Finally, this section reviews types of clergy sexual misconduct ranging from sexual harassment, pedophilia, various sexual addictions, and problems with pornography. We conclude by differentiating the sexual predator—with numerous victims—from onetime sexual misconduct usually growing out of a sense of deep personal depletion. The group brainstorms how religious leaders might best handle both types of cases of clergy sexual misconduct.

PART 3: WHY ARE BOUNDARIES SO DIFFICULT TO MAINTAIN?

Part 3 reviews what boundaries are and then asks the questions: "Why are boundaries so hard to maintain? Why is it so hard to say 'no' to things we really do not want to do in order to say 'yes' to things we are passionate about?"

In this section, we look at three aspects of what makes boundaries difficult to maintain:

1. *Issues of the self.* The psychoanalytic contributions of Carl Jung and Heinz Kohut are reviewed.

   - From Jung's perspective, the problem of the God complex for clergy is discussed in some depth and how it is possible for clergy to over-function to such an extent that they develop a savior complex.
   - From Kohut's perspective, the need for validation and affirmation as well as the need to be liked is discussed as a way of explaining why it is so hard to say "no." If clergy need to be liked and need validation, they may over-function in order to gain more validation. Examples and discussion questions help participants begin to realize how their deep yearning for affirmation and

need to be liked can drive them to both burnout and
misconduct.

2. *Issues of the anxious congregational system.* Clergy do not
   function in a vacuum. Rather, they function in systems that
   actually resent boundaries and in this sense help to cocreate
   boundary problems.

   - General systems theory is used to understand how sys-
     tems function, as well as how chronic anxiety impacts
     system functioning.
   - In particular, the implications of systems theory for
     anxious mainline congregations is discussed, and par-
     ticipants spend time brainstorming how their anxious
     congregations function and the pressure they absorb
     from their immersion in anxious systems.

3. *Issues of a self that needs validation and interacts with a
   chronically anxious system.* When clergy needs for validation
   interact with anxious systems, the result can be both burnout
   and boundary problems.

PART 4: PREVENTION

The workshop ends with a focus on prevention and how to set
boundaries that result in greater ministerial health and excellence.
   Three areas are examined:

1. Murray Bowen's systems-theory concept of "differentiation"
   is introduced and applied to clergy with the understanding
   that boundaries can only be set effectively when levels of
   differentiation are improved.

2. The notion of differentiation of self is expanded to include the concept of "emotional intelligence" and to help clergy take more practical steps toward setting clear boundaries while staying connected to parishioners.

3. The role of clergy groups in prevention is explored. Clergy groups can be a resource for deepening differentiation of self and emotional intelligence. In addition, they provide great support for clergy dealing with anxious congregations.

Appendix 2

TIPS FOR HOW TO ORGANIZE A CLERGY GROUP

1. Decide if you want to invite participants from one denomination or from multiple denominations. There are pros and cons both ways. Most participants rate the group with multiple denominations as a richer learning environment.

2. Consider the benefits and liabilities of mixing clergy at different points in their careers. An argument can be made either way, but we suggest being intentional about your choice. To focus on midcareer clergy, for example, may mean the participants can go deeper into the satisfactions and dissatisfactions of being in ministry over the long haul. Entering clergy have different concerns and struggles with boundaries. If you organize a mixed group, appeal to the ways in which the group members can learn from one another.

3. Use the "practice" questions at the end of each chapter to structure the group. Nothing kills a clergy group faster than it devolving into a complaint session. A trained facilitator can help keep the group on track and challenge and support members as needed. Most local pastoral counseling centers will have staff members available to lead clergy groups, and often

denominational leaders will also have a list of people available to facilitate these groups.

4. Consider ways in which group members can be accountable to and with one another for their individual and group learning experience—for example, by writing group and individual covenants.

More information about leading clergy groups can be found in these resources: *So Much Better: How Thousands of Pastors Help Each Other Thrive* and *Know Your Story and Lead with It: The Power of Narrative in Clergy Leadership*. Parker Palmer's guide to creating circles of trust, while not directly about clergy groups, provides very useful ideas for structuring a group.[1]

NOTES

I. THE PROBLEM WITH BOUNDARIES

1. Robert Frost, "Mending Wall," *The Poetry of Robert Frost*, ed. Edward Connery Lathem (New York: Holt, Rinehart and Winston, 1969), 33.

2. Ibid., 305.

3. Diana R. Garland and Christen Argueta, "How Clergy Sexual Misconduct Happens: A Qualitative Study of First-Hand Accounts," *Social Work and Christianity*, 37, no. 1 (2010): 1–27.

4. Mark Chaves and Diana Garland, "The Prevalence of Clergy Sexual Advances toward Adults in Their Congregations," *Journal for the Scientific Study of Religion* 48, no. 4 (2009): 817–24.

5. Diana R. Garland, "The Prevalence of Clergy Sexual Misconduct with Adults: A Research Study Executive Summary," Baylor University, accessed September 23, 2013, www.baylor.edu/clergysexualmisconduct.

6. Garland and Argueta, "How Clergy Sexual Misconduct Happens," 1–27.

7. Chaves and Garland, "The Prevalence of Clergy Sexual Advances," 821.

8. Ibid., 820.

9. Garland and Argueta, "How Clergy Sexual Misconduct Happens," 2.

10. S. P. Daniel and M. Rogers, "Burn-out and the Pastorate: A Critical Review with Implications for Pastors," *Journal of Psychology and Theology* 9, no. 3 (1981): 232–49.

11. Benjamin R. Doolittle, "Burnout and Coping among Parish-Based Clergy," *Mental Health, Religion and Culture* 10, no. 1 (January 2007): 31–38.

12. Perry C. Francis and Tracy D. Baldo, "Narcissistic Measures of Lutheran Clergy Who Self-Reported Committing Sexual Misconduct," *Pastoral Psychology* 47, no. 2 (1998): 81–96.

13. Peter L. Steinke, *Congregational Leadership in Anxious Times: Being Calm and Courageous No Matter What* (Herndon, VA: Alban, 2006).

14. Herbert J. Freudenberger, "Staff Burnout," *Journal of Social Issues*, 30, no. 1 (1974): 159–65.

15. William James, *The Varieties of Religious Experience* (New York: Doubleday, 1902).

16. Doolittle, "Burnout and Coping among Parish-Based Clergy," 36.

17. S. Butler and S. Zelen, "Sexual Intimacies between Psychotherapists and Their Patients," *Psychotherapy: Theory, Research, and Practice* (1977): 139, 143–44. Quoted in J. Thoburn and R. Baker, *Clergy Sexual Misconduct: A Systems Approach to Prevention, Intervention, and Oversight* (Carefree, AZ: Gentle Path Press, 2011), 10.

18. Daniel and Rogers, "Burn-out and the Pastorate," 233.

19. Timothy Lytton, "Clergy Sexual Abuse Litigation: The Policymaking Role of Tort Law," *Connecticut Law Review*, 39 no. 3 (2007): 809.

20. Garland and Argueta, "How Clergy Sexual Misconduct Happens," 1.

2. HEALTHY SELVES AND BOUNDARIES

1. Terry D. Cooper and Robert L. Randall, *Grace for the Injured Self: The Healing Approach of Heinz Kohut* (Eugene, OR: Pickwick, 2011), 2.

2. Henri J. M. Nouwen, *The Wounded Healer: Ministry in Contemporary Society* (New York: Doubleday, 1990), 90.

3. C. G. Jung, *Analytic Psycholog: Its Theory and Practice* (New York: Pantheon, 1968).

4. Valerie Saiving, "The Human Situation: A Feminine View," in *Woman Spirit Rising: A Feminist Reader in Religion*, ed. Carol P. Christ and Judith Plaskow (New York: HarperCollins, 1992), 25–42.

5. Sheryl Sandberg, *Lean In: Women, Work, and the Will to Lead* (New York: Knopf, 2013).

6. Nouwen, *The Wounded Healer*, 87.

3. SETTING BOUNDARIES IN ANXIOUS CONGREGATIONAL SYSTEMS

1. Ludwig von Bertalanffy, *General Systems Theory* (New York: George Braziller, 1968).

2. Urie Bronfenbrenner, *The Ecology of Human Development* (Cambridge, MA: Harvard University Press, 1979).

3. Michael E. Kerr and Murray Bowen, *Family Evaluation: An Approach Based on Bowen Theory* (New York: Norton, 1988).

4. Edwin H. Friedman, *Generation to Generation: Family Process in Church and Synagogue* (New York: Guilford, 1985); Edwin H. Friedman, *A Failure of Nerve: Leadership in the Age of the Quick Fix* (New York: Seabury Books, 1999); Ronald W. Richardson, *Creating a Healthier Church: Family Systems Theory, Leadership, and Congregational Life* (Minneapolis: Fortress, 1996).

5. Kerr, *Family Evaluation*, 7.

6. Ibid.

5. SAYING NO TO SAY YES

1. David Brooks, "The Leadership Revival," *New York Times*, January 14, 2014.

2. Malcolm Gladwell, *Outliers: The Story of Success* (New York: Back Bay Books, 2008), 40.

3. Daniel Levitin, *This Is Your Brain on Music: The Science of a Human Obsession* (New York: Dutton, 2006), 197.

4. Craig Dykstra, "On Our Way: Living into God's Future" (presentation, Indianapolis, May 11–13, 2011).

5. Ibid.

6. L. Gregory Jones and Kevin R. Armstrong, *Resurrecting Excellence: Shaping Faithful Christian Ministry* (Grand Rapids, MI: Eerdmans, 2006), 1.

7. Ibid., 41.

8. Jackson W. Carroll, *God's Potters: Pastoral Leadership and the Shaping of Congregations* (Grand Rapids, MI: Eerdmans, 2006).

9. "Sustaining Pastoral Excellence," Lilly Endowment, accessed March 18, 2014, www.lillyendowment.org/religion_spe.html.

10. Austin Presbyterian Seminary College of Pastoral Leaders, "A Study of the Effects of Participation in SPE Pastoral Leader Peer Groups: Survey Report and Analysis," April 2010, 4–6.

11. Ibid., 10.

12. Ibid., 22.

13. Ibid., 21.

14. Ibid., 30.

15. Friedman, *Generation to Generation*; Friedman, *A Failure of Nerve*; Steinke, *Congregational Leadership*; Peter L. Steinke, *Healthy Congregations: A Systems Approach* (Herndon, VA: Alban 1996).

16. Kerr and Bowen, *Family Evaluation*, 145.

17. Murray Bowen, *Family Therapy in Clinical Practice* (New York: Jason Aronson, 1978).

18. Daniel Goleman, *Emotional Intelligence: Why It Can Matter More than IQ* (New York: Bantam, 2006).

19. Friedman, *Failure of Nerve.*
20. Goleman, *Emotional Intelligence,* 84.
21. Ibid.
22. Austin Presbyterian Seminary College of Pastoral Leaders, "A Study of the Effects of Participation in SPE Pastoral Leader Peer Groups," 28.
23. Friedman, *Failure of Nerve.*
24. Margaret J. Marcuson, *Leaders Who Last: Sustaining Yourself and Your Ministry* (New York: Seabury, 2009).
25. Basil M. Pennington, *Centering Prayer: Renewing an Ancient Christian Prayer Form* (New York: Image Books, 1982); Thomas Keating, *Open Mind, Open Heart: The Contemplative Dimension of the Gospel* (New York: Continuum, 2006).
26. Serene Jones, "Graced Practices: Excellence and Freedom in the Christian Life," in *Practicing Theology: Beliefs and Practices in Christian Life,* ed. Miroslav Volf and Dorothy Bass (Grand Rapids, MI: Eerdmans, 2002), 51–77.
27. Ibid., 52.
28. Ibid., 66.

APPENDIX 2. TIPS FOR HOW TO ORGANIZE A CLERGY GROUP

1. Richard L. Hester and Kelli Walker-Jones, *Know Your Story and Lead with It: The Power of Narrative in Clergy Leadership* (Herndon, VA: Alban Institute, 2009); Parker J. Palmer, *A Hidden Wholeness: The Journey toward an Undivided Life* (San Francisco: Jossey-Bass, 2004).

BIBLIOGRAPHY

Bowen, Murray. *Family Therapy in Clinical Practice*. New York: Jason Aronson, 1978.

Bronfenbrenner, Urie. *The Ecology of Human Development*. Cambridge, MA: Harvard University Press, 1979.

Butler, S., and Zelen, S. "Sexual Intimacies between Psychotherapists and Their Patients." *Psychotherapy: Theory, Research, and Practice* (1977): 139, 143–44. Quoted in Thoburn, J., and Baker, R. *Clergy Sexual Misconduct: A Systems Approach to Prevention, Intervention, and Oversight*. Carefree, AZ: Gentle Path Press, 2011.

Carroll, Jackson W. *God's Potters: Pastoral Leadership and the Shaping of Congregations*. Grand Rapids, MI: Eerdmans, 2006.

Chaves, Mark, and Diana Garland. "The Prevalence of Clergy Sexual Advances toward Adults in Their Congregations." *Journal for the Scientific Study of Religion* 48, no. 4 (2009): 817–24.

Cooper, Terry D., and Robert L. Randall. *Grace for the Injured Self: The Healing Approach of Heinz Kohut*. Eugene, OR: Pickwick, 2011.

Daniel, S. P., and M. Rogers. "Burn-out and the Pastorate: A Critical Review with Implications for Pastors." *Journal of Psychology and Theology* 9, no. 3 (1981): 232–49.

Doolittle, Benjamin R. "Burnout and Coping among Parish-Based Clergy." *Mental Health, Religion and Culture* 10, no. 1 (January 2007): 31–38.

Francis, Perry C., and Tracy D. Baldo. "Narcissistic Measures of Lutheran Clergy Who Self-Reported Committing Sexual Misconduct." *Pastoral Psychology* 47, no. 2 (1998): 81–96.

Freudenberger, Herbert J. "Staff Burnout." *Journal of Social Issues* 30, no. 1 (1974): 159–65.

Friedman, Edwin H. *A Failure of Nerve: Leadership in the Age of the Quick Fix*. New York: Seabury Books, 1999.

———. *Generation to Generation: Family Process in Church and Synagogue*. New York: Guilford, 1985.

Frost, Robert. *The Poetry of Robert Frost.* Edited by Edward Connery Lathem. New York: Holt, Rinehart and Winston, 1969.

Garland, Diana R. "The Prevalence of Clergy Sexual Misconduct with Adults: A Research Study Executive Summary." Baylor University. Accessed September 23, 2013. www.baylor.edu/clergysexualmisconduct.

Garland, Diana R., and Christen Argueta. "How Clergy Sexual Misconduct Happens: A Qualitative Study of First-Hand Accounts." *Social Work and Christianity* 37, no. 1 (2010): 1–27.

Gladwell, Malcolm. *Outliers: The Story of Success.* New York: Back Bay Books, 2008.

Goleman, Daniel. *Emotional Intelligence: Why It Can Matter More than IQ.* New York: Bantam, 2006.

Hester, Richard L., and Walker-Jones, Kelli. *Know Your Story and Lead with It: The Power of Narrative in Clergy Leadership.* Herndon, VA: Alban Institute, 2009.

James, William. *The Varieties of Religious Experience.* New York: Doubleday, 1902.

Jones, L. Gregory, and Kevin R. Armstrong. *Resurrecting Excellence: Shaping Faithful Christian Ministry.* Grand Rapids, MI: Eerdmans, 2006.

Jones, Serene. "Graced Practices: Excellence and Freedom in the Christian Life." In *Practicing Theology: Beliefs and Practices in Christian Life,* edited by Miroslav Volf and Dorothy Bass, 51–77. Grand Rapids, MI: Eerdmans, 2002.

Jung, C. G. *Analytic Psycholog: Its Theory and Practice.* New York: Pantheon, 1968.

Keating, Thomas. *Open Mind, Open Heart: The Contemplative Dimension of the Gospel.* New York: Continuum, 2006.

Kerr, Michael E., and Murray Bowen. *Family Evaluation: An Approach Based on Bowen Theory.* New York: Norton, 1988.

Levitin, Daniel. *This Is Your Brain on Music: The Science of a Human Obsession.* New York: Dutton, 2006.

Lytton, Timothy. "Clergy Sexual Abuse Litigation: The Policymaking Role of Tort Law." *Connecticut Law Review,* 39, no. 3 (2007): 809–95.

Marcuson, Margaret J. *Leaders Who Last: Sustaining Yourself and Your Ministry.* New York: Seabury, 2009.

Nouwen, Henri J. M. *The Wounded Healer: Ministry in Contemporary Society.* New York: Doubleday, 1990.

Palmer, Parker J. *A Hidden Wholeness: The Journey toward an Undivided Life.* San Francisco: Jossey-Bass, 2004.

Pennington, Basil M. *Centering Prayer: Renewing an Ancient Christian Prayer Form.* New York: Image Books, 1982.

Richardson, Ronald W. *Creating a Healthier Church: Family Systems Theory, Leadership, and Congregational Life.* Minneapolis: Fortress, 1996.

Saiving, Valerie. "The Human Situation: A Feminine View." In *Womanspirit Rising: A Feminist Reader in Religion,* edited by Carol P. Christ and Judith Plaskow, 25–42. New York: HarperCollins, 1992.

Sandberg, Sheryl. *Lean In: Women, Work, and the Will to Lead.* New York: Knopf, 2013.

Steinke, Peter L. *Congregational Leadership in Anxious Times: Being Calm and Courageous No Matter What.* Herndon, VA: Alban, 2006.

————. *Healthy Congregations: A Systems Approach*. Herndon, VA: Alban 1996.

Sustaining Pastoral Excellence Peer Learning Project. *So Much Better: How Thousands of Pastors Help Each Other Thrive*. St. Louis, MO: Chalice Press, 2013.

von Bertalanffy, Ludwig. *General Systems Theory*. New York: George Braziller, 1968.

ABOUT THE AUTHORS

David C. Olsen is executive director of the Samaritan Counseling Center of the Capital Region and an adjunct faculty member of the Sage Graduate School. He has been presenting on "Boundary Awareness Training for Clergy" for the past fourteen years. His books include *The Spiritual Work of Marriage*, *The Couple's Survival Workbook*, and *When Helping Starts to Hurt.*

Nancy G. Devor is senior staff psychologist at the Danielsen Institute at Boston University. She previously served as vice president for the Samaritan Institute in Denver, Colorado. She is a contributor to the book *Aging, Spirituality and Religion*, the *Journal of Pastoral Care*, and the *Journal of Pastoral Psychology.*

Made in the USA
Monee, IL
20 October 2020

45710937R00083